MODELER'S GUIDE TO THE RIGHT OF WAY

By Jeff Wilson

Kalmbach
Media

On the cover: A freight rolls westbound behind a 2-8-2 Mikado on Baltimore & Ohio's double-track main line across Indiana in the early 1950s. *Linn H. Westcott*

Back cover: From left: The difference in ballast between the main line and passing siding—tall stone on the main, low cinders on the siding—is apparent on the Illinois Central Gulf near Litchfield, Ill., in 1971. *J. David Ingles;* EMD FTs lead the *Cascadian* along stacks of new tie plates and wooden spike kegs (at left), signaling an upcoming track improvement project in May 1953. *George Krambles; Krambles-Peterson Archive;* A Soo Line freight is looking at a red-yellow-red (diverging approach) signal, which tells the crew it's taking a siding at restricted speed at Grayslake, Ill. *Jim Hediger*

Kalmbach Media
21027 Crossroads Circle
Waukesha, Wisconsin 53186
www.KalmbachHobbyStore.com

Published in 2022
26 25 24 23 22   1 2 3 4 5

Manufactured in China

ISBN: 978-1-62700-911-9
EISBN: 978-1-62700-912-6

Editor: Eric White
Book Design: Lisa Bergman

Library of Congress Control Number: 2022933216

Contents

Signs along a weed-grown Milwaukee Road track near Milwaukee in 1973 include a flanger post (black flags on a reflective white background on a wood post) and a crossing alert. *Gordon Odegard*

Introduction

The railroad right of way is a fascinating place, filled with a lot more than the track itself. Thousands of details lurk there, waiting to be modeled. Knowing what these various elements are, how they're used, and how they've evolved will lead to more accurate and realistic model railroad scenes.

"Right of way" literally means "right to make a way over a parcel of land." Most railroads received their rights to exist from government grants, giving them ownership of a path through federal- or state-owned land. Railroads can also acquire land for their track through eminent domain via state or federal laws.

A railroad's physical right of way is usually 100 feet wide, measured 50 feet outward from the center of the track. This can be narrower, especially in urban areas, and it was sometimes wider (the General Railroad Right of Way Act of 1875 allowed railroads to claim a 200-foot-wide path across public lands).

The most noticeable component of the right of way is the track itself. The rails and ties provide a surprising amount of variations. Track details include turnouts of many types, crossings, and all related connectors and components such as joint bars, spikes, switch stands, switch machines, switch heaters, derails, guardrails, and wood and concrete ties.

The roadbed and subroadbed are key elements. Elevating the track above the surrounding ground controls grades and provides drainage and stability. This includes the ballast, sub-ballast, and subgrade, including fills and cuts to allow the line to smoothly go through hills and valleys.

Highway and street crossings provide a wealth of details, including the crossings themselves, along with warning signs, gates, and crossing signals.

There are many other details along the tracks. These include pole lines (for communication, signaling, and power), various types of signals and signal bridges, equipment cases, battery vaults, phone boxes, defect detectors, signs, microwave towers, antennas, retaining walls, and fences.

Many of these details have evolved significantly since the early 1900s. Adding these details helps transform a layout from simply "track" to a representation of a prototype right of way. To be realistic, however, you can't simply add them at random: the more you know about prototype rights of way, the better you'll be able to create a realistic layout.

Turn the page and we'll start with a look at the most basic element of a right of way: the track itself.

There's a lot of detail in this view along the right of way of the Union Pacific east of Julesburg, Colo., in 2003: the wide, four-track roadway; the taller profile of the two main (center) tracks compared to the outside tracks; the signal bridge with its multiple color-light signals; and the equipment cases, signs, and signals along the tracks in the distance. Oh, and the westbound train is pretty cool, too. *Jeff Wilson*

Ed Theisinger

CHAPTER ONE

Track structure

Any detailed look at the railroad right of way must begin with the track itself. The track structure—rails, ties, spikes, connectors—is critical for safe, smooth operation. These components have all evolved over the years, and their appearance varies by traffic levels. Knowing the details of prototype track is critical for capturing its appearance in a realistic manner on model railroads.

Chesapeake & Ohio's first Kanawha (2-8-4), no. 2700, lugs a westbound coal train at Catlettsburg, Ky., in May 1952. The C&O main line has jointed rail atop clean, gray ballast; note the spur track at right on the cinder subroadbed. Even though the track is well maintained, you can see the downward depressions at the rail joints, caused by the passing of thousands of coal cars.

Not all track is well maintained. The jointed rail and turnouts in the Rock Island yard at Dallas, Texas, in 1977 is definitely slow-speed territory. Note the lack of ballast, as the track has sunk into the ground. *Lee Langum*

Early rail was often secured to stones instead of wooden ties. This is from a stretch of Camden & South Amboy dating to the 1830s, with 40-pound T-rail (rolled in England). The C&SA became part of the Pennsylvania Railroad. *Pennsylvania Railroad; courtesy Association of American Railroads*

EARLY RAIL CROSS SECTIONS

CAST IRON RAIL	CAST IRON EDGE RAIL	ROBERT L. STEVENS TEE-RAIL	U OR BRIDGE RAIL	FIRST U.S. TEE-RAIL	FIRST BESSEMER RAIL ROLLED IN U.S.
1808	1816	1831	1835	1845	1865

Many styles of iron rail were tried before modern steel T-rail appeared in the mid-1860s. *Bethlehem Steel Co.*

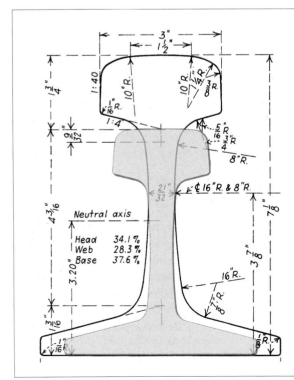

RAIL HEIGHT VARIATIONS

Rail height varies by weight. The shaded rail is 90-pound ARA-A rail (5-3/8") and the tall rail is 132-pound RE rail (7-1/8"), which is also about an inch wider at the base. *American Railway Association*

Gauge

The standard track gauge (the width between inside edges of the railheads) in North America is 4'-8½", but the early days of railroading saw railroads using a wide variety of gauges. Five feet was common in Southern states, with 6 feet on some Northern lines—notably the Erie. Many narrow gauge lines were built with gauges of 2 feet (primarily in Maine) and 3 feet.

As railroad mileage grew and equipment became larger, more and more labor was required to transload freight between railcars of competing railroads with differing gauges. The importance of being able to exchange freight cars became apparent, and a movement began to unify track gauge among railroads.

The current standard gauge was effectively established with the Pacific

Railway Act of 1862, which chartered the first transcontinental railroad. Construction began the following year, and was completed in 1869. Although most northern lines adjusted to match this, many railroads in the South remained at 5 feet for another two decades. It wasn't until 1886 when these lines agreed to change, a project largely accomplished over two days (May 31-June 1) of that year.

Most narrow gauge lines were abandoned or converted to standard gauge by 1900, but they remained in some areas, primarily in the Rocky Mountains and Maine.

Components

There's a lot more to the design of rails, ties, and other components than is first apparent. The nature of steel wheels on steel rails creates high dynamic forces, as each wheel of a modern freight car delivers nearly 18 tons of pressure to the railhead on an area smaller than a dime. And that's standing still—add forces that cause cars to rock and wheels to move laterally, or factor in the forces of a train in motion on a curve, and the stresses greatly increase.

To handle this stress, track must be slightly flexible: its components must allow some movement under load to distribute forces (watch a train roll along, and you'll see deflection of the rail under the wheels). Track also must be firm: too much flexion and individual components can crack or develop fatigue, or the track can become unstable.

As railroad equipment has evolved and become larger and heavier and train speeds increased, track components have likewise grown and evolved to handle the increased weights and forces. Let's start with a look at each of the track components.

Rail has evolved substantially since the 1800s, increasing in size as loads have become heavier. And although it can't be seen, it has changed with advances in metallurgy and steel production to be produced with the best composition for hardness and resistance to wear and stress.

The first rails of the early 1800s were iron straps fastened to

MODELING TIP

Model rail sizes: Breaking the "code"

Regardless of scale, rail size for model track is specified by "code." This isn't a top-secret formula: code simply refers to the height of the rail in thousandths of an inch. Thus code 83 track has rail .083" tall, code 70 is .070" tall, and so on. The accompanying chart lists common rail sizes in each scale, along with the corresponding prototype rail each represents. Note that some model track scales out to be extremely heavy (code 100 in HO is oversize for almost all prototype rail; code 80 in N is grossly oversize for all prototypes). Using different sizes is a good way to differentiate the apparent purpose of model track: for example, in HO, using code 83 for the main line and code 70 for spurs and sidings.

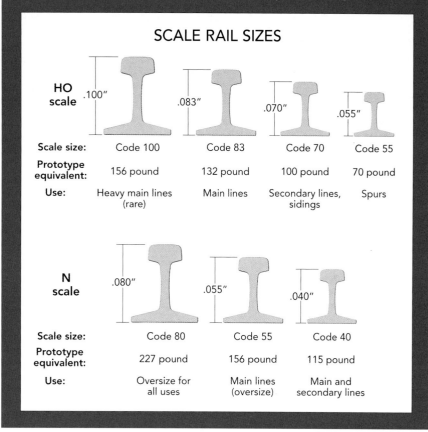

SCALE RAIL SIZES

HO scale

	.100"	.083"	.070"	.055"

Scale size:	Code 100	Code 83	Code 70	Code 55
Prototype equivalent:	156 pound	132 pound	100 pound	70 pound
Use:	Heavy main lines (rare)	Main lines	Secondary lines, sidings	Spurs

N scale

	.080"	.055"	.040"

Scale size:	Code 80	Code 55	Code 40
Prototype equivalent:	227 pound	156 pound	115 pound
Use:	Oversize for all uses	Main lines (oversize)	Main and secondary lines

longitudinal timbers. Even with the light equipment of the early 1800s, this didn't work well, as the iron straps tended to separate from the timbers and curl up as cars passed over them, often with disastrous results if the straps broke into the car interiors.

The solution was solid iron rails with a T-shaped cross-section, which first appeared in England in 1831 and were first rolled in U.S. mills in 1845. The first steel rails began appearing in 1865.

The basic rail shape, or cross-section, has remained similar since the mid-1800s. The large, flat bottom

is the base; the vertical section is the web, and the wide part at the top upon which the wheels ride is the head. The size of the rail has increased substantially, with heavier (wider and taller) rail able to support heavier loads and faster train speeds.

Rail size is rated by weight, in pounds per yard. Early rail was light, only 36 to 60 pounds per yard. By 1900, mainline rail was typically 90 pounds, with 112-pound rail by the mid-1930s. In 1921, the average rail weight on Class 1 railroads was 82.8 pounds; by 1956 it was 105 pounds.

The Soo Line main line at right has a taller profile and heavier, welded rail compared to the lighter, jointed-rail passing siding at left. The spur at left likely has even lighter rail, and lacks ballast. The view of Lomira, Wis., is from the fireman's seat of a diesel in 1982. *Jim Hediger*

Rail at 132 pounds was used on heavy-traffic lines by the 1940s, and the Pennsylvania Railroad was noted for its massive 152-pound rail that it began using on some routes in the 1930s. Today, most mainline rail is 136 or 141 pounds, but there is still plenty of lighter rail on secondary lines, branch lines, passing sidings, and industrial tracks.

The tremendous growth in the North American rail network and expansion of lines from the late 1800s into the 1900s meant there was a huge market for new rail, and by the 1890s, manufacturers were producing rail in 119 different profiles and 27 weights. Rail designs were eventually standardized under the direction of the American Railway Association (ARA) starting in 1905 (the American Association of Railroads after 1934).

Differences in rail profiles include depth of the head and width of the web and base. As modelers, we don't have to concern ourselves with that, but we need to be aware of the most-visible spotting feature of rail: the height. The drawing on page 6 shows the dimensions for 132-pound rail, which is noticeably taller at 7⅛" than the 90-pound (5⅝" tall) shown with it. Modern 141 pound RE rail is 7⁷⁄₁₆" tall.

This contrast in rail heights is noticeable when looking at prototype track side by side, such as where a spur or passing track is near a main line. Modelers can capture this look by using heavier rail for main lines and lighter rail for other areas—in HO, for

Prototype rail lettering

Rail is labeled when it is produced, with standard notation to indicate basic information. The lettering on this rail, from left to right, includes size/weight (112 pound); type ("RE," a profile standard of the American Railway Engineering Association, or AREA); mill production process ("OH," for "open hearth" method); manufacturer (Bethlehem Steel Co. Steelton Works); and date of manufacture (1934). This jointed rail is on a former secondary main line that by the 1990s had been shortened to an industrial branch.
Tom Nelligan

example, with code 83 rail for main lines and code 70 for spurs and sidings (see the chart on page 7).

The length of individual rail sections on prototype railroads has always been based on the length of standard gondola cars of each era. This meant 15- to 20-foot sections in the 1800s, extending to 33 feet by 1898. The common 39-foot length, adopted in 1925 and still found on railroads across the country, was designed to fit in a 40-foot gondola, and most new jointed rail was this size through the 1960s. Today, rail is typically offered in 70- and 80-foot sections, although 39-foot rail is still produced.

Jointed rail is easy to spot in photos as well as real life, with the joint bars and gaps usually accentuated by slight depressions in the rail at the joints. Small gaps at each joint, to allow for rail expansion and contraction, provide the familiar "clickity-clack" romanticized by many, but despised by railroads.

Railroads like to eliminate rail joints as much as possible, as joints are problematic in many ways: Wheels batter at rail ends as they cross joints, causing chipping, wear, and vertical deflection. This downward deflection is more pronounced at joints, especially where the joint isn't directly supported by a tie, causing wear to joint bars that can lead to cracking and breaking. The bolts on joint bars require periodic tightening. Along signaled lines, each joint requires a bond wire between

Union Pacific's double-track main in Nebraska features heavy welded rail. Even so, you can see the rails deflect under the wheels of loaded 286,000-pound coal gondolas in this 2006 view. *Jeff Wilson*

butted rails to ensure electrical conductivity.

All of these joint bars and bond wires (more on them in a bit) are big expenses for railroads, both in terms of materials as well as the labor to add and maintain them. As an example, every mile of track with conventional 39-foot lengths of rail has 270 rail joints—135 on each rail—which means 540 joint bars, 2,160 bolts, and 270 bond wires to be installed and maintained.

Welded rail

The ultimate solution to the problem of rail joints is continuous welded rail (CWR), also called "ribbon rail." It's made by welding together individual sections of rail into quarter-mile-long pieces, which are then carried to installation locations on special rack cars that hold multiple lengths of rail (see Welded Rail Train on page 11). Once laid, the rail is then field-welded to even longer stretches—often

Railroads regularly replace ties as needed, as shown by these discarded ties along the tracks in 1973. They will be picked up by a work crew and recycled, repurposed, or burned. *Gordon Odegard*

A large stack of new, freshly treated ties sits along the tracks awaiting installation in 1973. *Gordon Odegard*

Concrete ties have a stepped profile, and are lower in the middle than the ends. They are longer, wider, and spaced farther apart than wood ties, and use clips instead of spikes to secure the rail. *Jeff Wilson*

The ties along this industrial lead track are more widely spaced than on a main line. They vary widely in appearance in size as well as color, from light gray to medium and dark brown. *Jeff Wilson*

(Right) In the steam era, some secondary track was laid without tie plates. This rail, on the Monon in the 1940s, shows the results, with rail cutting down severely into some of the ties. The joint bar is a standard four-bolt design. *Linn H. Westcott*

several miles, with the length generally determined by the length of signal blocks or distance between turnouts.

Along with lowered maintenance costs in both labor and materials, railroads quickly discovered that CWR significantly improves operations. It provides a smoother ride with less wear and damage to rolling stock, loads, and locomotives from wheels hitting rail joints, allowing higher train speeds in many cases.

The first CWR on mainline railroads appeared in 1933, although some railroads had experimented with shorter lengths of welded rail earlier (mainly in station areas, street trackage, and on interurban lines). The Central of Georgia was the first to install a significant length on mainline track—through a couple of tunnels—and

Delaware & Hudson followed with 42 miles of CWR through the 1930s. Welded rail remained relatively rare through the 1950s, with less than 1,000 total miles in service by 1955. Tunnels were popular initial locations, along with long bridges and other areas where routine track maintenance can be difficult.

The main challenges in laying welded rail were developing effective methods for welding the butt ends of rail, then controlling the long rail's expansion and contraction caused by changes in temperature, which can be extreme (120 degrees or more) in some areas. This can cause rail to fracture (or pull apart joints) in extreme cold and buckle or kink in extreme heat. Learning to control this is the main reason it took 30-plus years for CWR

to become common.

To combat this, rail is pre-stressed (heated and cooled in a controlled manner), and then installed at a "rail-neutral" temperature to avoid extreme forces in either direction. This is usually about 30 to 40 degrees below the maximum rail temperature at the installation location, keeping the rail in slight tension at most times.

The other key is to anchor CWR more securely than standard rail—concrete ties are often used—and give track a deeper ballast profile. Firmer anchoring keeps the rail in place and prevents it from moving lengthwise once installed. Improvements in welding (thermite welding is now standard), along with stronger joint bars and connectors at the end sections of CWR (particularly insulated joints)

A Southern Pacific crew unloads 1,512-foot lengths of welded rail from a rack train. Once the rails are in place, they'll be field-welded into even longer sections. *Southern Pacific*

Welded rail train

Welded rail is transported from the factory to location on quarter-mile-long trains of special rack cars that carry up to 40 strings of rail in four layers. Roller stands at each rail location allow for loading and unloading. The rail is clamped securely at one car in the center of the train. This keeps the rail from shifting, but allows for movement through the other cars' roller stands as the train negotiates curves. The rail is flexible enough to bend as directed when unloading it, either directly to the ties or, in some cases, next to the track for later installation.

have increased reliability.

As technology advanced, CWR mileage increased considerably beginning in the late 1950s. The first year that saw more than 1,000 miles of CWR installed was 1959; by the 1970s, railroads were adding 4,000 to 6,000 miles of CWR annually. Total CWR mileage in 1976 was about 60,000; by the 2000s it was over 100,000 miles, with most major main lines equipped.

Rail maintenance

The fracture or failure of rail can cause derailments and severe damage. Rail failure can be caused by flaws in the rail, damage and wear from passing trains, or a combination of reasons. Railroads had to rely on visual inspection to catch problems into the 1920s. The problem is that many flaws can remain hidden within the rail.

The first rolling detector car, developed by Dr. Elmer A. Sperry, was built in 1928. While in motion, the car passes a current through the rail, setting up a magnetic field. Analyzing the field detects abnormal distortions, which indicate flaws in the rail. The company named after Sperry soon had a fleet of cars rolling on railroads across the country. Regular rail inspection is now mandated, and other companies

This modern track has double-shoulder tie plates with separate spike holes for mounting the plate and securing the rail. Rail anchors are placed around every other tie. *TRAINS magazine collection*

(including Herzog and DAPCO) now operate detector cars.

Regular rail maintenance includes rail grinding, which restores the rail profile and surface and removes surface imperfections. Rail wear is significant on busy railroads, with some areas requiring rail replacement every year or two, so railroads do all they can to extend rail life.

Rail is regularly reused. Rail that's

removed from one location and reinstalled in another is called "relay" rail. This can include rail from a main line that's been downgraded being moved to another main line, or worn mainline rail being reinstalled in a siding or spur. Rail on secondary lines, branch lines, and industrial spurs can have long life—there's plenty of rail rolled in the early 1900s that's still in service.

Some railroads opt for longer, six-bolt joint bars on heavy-traffic lines. This joint, with composite-strand, tapered-pin bond wire, is on the Pennsylvania Railroad.
Roderick H. Craib Jr.

Multiple bond wires connect the rails at the joint on this secondary track. The tie plates are small, with the spike holes securing the rails as well as securing the plate to the tie. *TRAINS magazine collection*

Ties

Ties (crossties) perform several vital functions. As their name implies, they "tie" the rails together, keeping them aligned and in proper gauge. They support the weight of the rails and the loads they carry (cars and locomotives), providing a broad footprint to dissipate the force and spread it over a larger area. And they allow the track structure to be resilient, providing some "give" to the dynamic forces of moving trains.

Railroads use a lot of ties. How many? In 2020 alone, North American railroads purchased about 20.5 million wood ties, plus several hundred thousand concrete ties. With this expenditure, it benefits railroads and manufacturers alike to design ties that produce the best performance and longest possible lifespans.

The first railroads of the early 1800s had rails resting on stone bases, or sleepers (as they're still called in Europe). This didn't work well, as the stone was prone to shifting in the ground, causing misalignment. Railroads soon adopted wood timbers placed crosswise under the rails, which have been the standard ever since. Wood still retains 93 percent of the new-tie market, although concrete ties have become more popular since the 1980s. Other materials, including steel, resin, and composite (plastic-encapsulated wood) have been used, but in very small numbers.

Early untreated ties required frequent replacing, often lasting less than 10 years. By 1900 ties were pressure-treated with creosote, helping them withstand damage from water, insects, and decay. Exactly how long individual ties last in service depends upon the type of wood they're made from, the type of treatment they receive, the traffic level they support, and the ground and atmospheric conditions to which they're subjected. Ties in dry climates and ground conditions last longer than damp climates. There are ties still in service on secondary and branch lines that are 75 or more years old; even on heavy service lines, 30 to 40 years isn't unusual.

Railroads are continually upgrading individual ties as needed. You'll often see stacks of new ties awaiting installation along the right-of-way, and you'll also see old ties that have been removed laying along the side of the roadbed, awaiting pickup by a track gang. Tie removal into the 1950s was usually a labor-intensive practice, done with manual tools; recent decades have seen the growth of machines that can pull spikes, remove ties, put new ties in place, and spike them, all automatically.

New, freshly treated ties are nearly black in appearance. As ties age, they fade to medium and then light gray, often with brown highlights, depending upon the type of wood they're made from.

Many early ties were sawed or hewn

A light tap or two with a hammer and sturdy putty knife will create the effect of undulating track on an industrial spur. Go slowly and test equipment as you go to make sure the effect isn't too severe.
Two photos: Jeff Wilson

Distressing track

It's possible to capture the look of undulating, waving track as often seen in prototype industrial track and branch lines, where rail joints have become depressed. The key is to make sure that the modeled track stays in gauge. With slow-speed operations, models will usually operate just fine over such track (do not distress track at turnouts or crossings!). I do this by using a heavy chisel-style putty knife, giving it light taps with a hammer to depress the rail at simulated rail joints. Several light taps are much better than one heavy blow.

Ideally, do this when the track is initially laid, before adding ballast and scenery. As the photos show, it's also possible to do this after these things are in place. Experiment on a test section before doing it on your layout, and use care—test equipment as you go, since it's hard to reverse the process once it's done. I generally save this treatment for industrial spurs and other slow-speed track.

on two sides only (top and bottom), with widths that varied widely. Since the early 1900s, ties with all four sides sawed/hewn have been standard. Early ties were usually 8'-0" long; most modern ties are 8'-6" long, but some railroads prefer 9'-0" ties. Tie height and width vary from 5" to 7" tall and 5" to 10" wide, with sizes falling into numbered standard dimensions from No. 0 to No. 6 (see the chart on page 15). As train speeds and weights have increased, tie size has likewise increased, with No. 4 (7" x 8") and No. 5 (7" x 9") now the most common.

To stabilize ties and keep them from splitting, checking, or cracking, most ties have metal reinforcements on their ends called "tie irons" (also sometimes called "S irons" or "end plates"). These are sometimes metal shapes driven into the ends; they can also be spiked metal mesh driven onto the end. These devices began appearing in the 1940s, and are standard for most

new installations.

Tie spacing varies based on era, traffic, and loads. On modern main lines a 19.5" center-to-center spacing is typical, meaning about 3,250 ties per mile of track. Industrial spurs, yard tracks, sidings, branch lines, and older installations often have wider spacing. A contemporary Canadian National specification sheet for new industrial trackage calls for 20" spacing on lead tracks and 22" on body (storage or loading) tracks.

Concrete ties

Concrete ties are not a recent innovation—they were first tried by the Reading in a 200-tie test installation in 1893. Several other manufacturers and railroads designed, patented, and tested various designs in the early 1900s, but none made it past the experimental stage, mainly because concrete ties were significantly more expensive than wood versions, which

were readily available, cheap, and worked well.

By the late 1950s, rising prices of treated-wood products prompted a new look at the idea of concrete ties. At the urging of the Association of American Railroads (AAR), precast, prestressed concrete ties were developed and tested starting in 1957. Several designs were tried, with variations in tie shape and methods of securing rails.

As a tie material, concrete's positive attributes include overall strength; resistance to decay and deterioration from insects, water, and other weather factors; and the ability to manufacture them to specific, consistent dimensions and quality. The main challenge of concrete is its lack of flexibility, which can lead to cracking and abrasion; concrete ties also remain more expensive per unit than wood ties. The hope was that concrete ties would prove to be longer-lasting, countering their initial expense.

Compromise joint bars are tapered to join rails of differing size. They're commonly found on industrial spurs. *TRAINS magazine collection*

The first test sections of the new tie designs were installed on several railroads' main lines in 1960 and 1961 (on Atlantic Coast Line, Canadian National, St. Louis-San Francisco, and Seaboard Air Line). However, the ties quickly showed problems, primarily cracking (in the middle from flexing or under the rail seats) and wear/abrasion on the tie under the rails.

The best of the initial designs was modified, with changes including increasing the amount of prestress during casting and altering the tie profile, mainly by deepening the tie at the rail pads. The changes improved their durability, and by the late 1960s about a million concrete ties were in service in additional locations. Although reasonably successful, a high percentage suffered various failures (mainly cracking).

Insulated joint bars have non-conductive pads between the bars and rail, a spacer in the rail joint, and lined bolt holes. They're usually painted to indicate their location. *TRAINS magazine collection*

Manufacturers continued redesigning the ties, mounting pads, and rail clips, leading to improved performance. Installations stepped up by the 1980s and later, and as of 2020 more than 35 million concrete ties were in use on North American railroads. Although wood ties still dominate the market, concrete—with about 6 percent of total market share—has become the choice for many railroads for their heavy-haul and high-speed traffic lines. They are not perfect, and still fail on occasion due to various cracking issues as well as chemical degradation and abrasion under the rail seats.

Modern concrete ties are wider than wood ties (11" compared to 8" or 9"), are long (9 feet), and allow wider spacing: 24" to 30" center to center. This mitigates the initial expense somewhat, since several hundred fewer ties are required per mile compared to wood. The Railway Tie Association estimates that overall installation costs per mile for wood ties is 60 to 80 percent of concrete.

Other materials have been used for ties with limited success. Steel ties are economical, stable, and don't require separate tie plates, but on signaled lines require insulation. Resin (cast) and composite (wood sealed in plastic) ties have also been offered by some manufacturers. All of these types together, however, account for well under 1 percent of the total tie market.

Fasteners and hardware

Rails were initially spiked directly atop the wood crossties. As cars and locomotives became heavier, this arrangement proved unsatisfactory, as the base of the rails would dig into the wood ties over time, often skewing and losing alignment as well. The solution was the tie plate, a steel plate that fits atop the tie between it and the rail base. The top has longitudinal ridges that keep the rail aligned, with square holes next to the rail allowing spikes to pass through while keeping them in alignment as well.

Tie plates are made in several sizes to match the many types of rail in service. In general, the heavier the rail

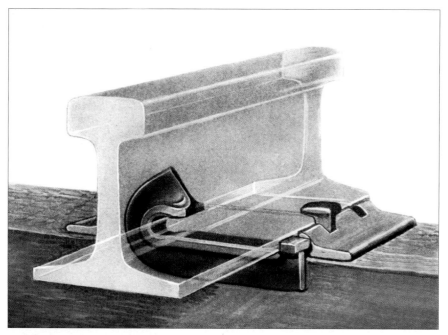

Rail anchors prevent rail from creeping lengthwise. They lock around the base of the rail next to the tie. They have been made in many styles; this is an Improved Fair Rail Anchor from the P&M Company, circa late 1940s. *P&M Co.*

Prototype tie dimensions

Since the early 1900s, wood ties have been made to specific standard sizes, specified by number. Each of the standard ties can be 8'-0", 8'-6", or 9'-0" long. They're listed by dimension (thickness x width):

No. 0: 5 x 5
No. 1: 6 x 6
No. 2: 6 x 7
No. 3: 6 x 8
No. 4: 7 x 8
No. 5: 7 x 9
No. 6: 7 x 10

Railroads use rail braces—the triangular fixtures on the outside of the near rail—where rail is subject to lateral forces. They're common on turnouts, but also sometimes on curves on mainline track, as here on the Illinois Central in the late 1950s. *William D. Middleton*

Great Northern's main line on Stevens Pass in Washington was well-maintained with smooth trackwork and sharp ballast profile. Here FTs lead the *Cascadian* along stacks of new tie plates and wooden spike kegs (at left), signaling an upcoming track improvement project in May 1953. *George Krambles; Krambles-Peterson Archive*

 MODELING TIP

Painting and detailing rail and ties

Among the easiest details you can add to increase track realism are joint bars; in this case every 39 feet for a steam to early diesel era layout. Joint bars have been offered in HO scale from Details West, KV Models, PDC, and others; adding them is as simple as gluing them to the rail web. I only add joint bars on the sides of the rails easily seen by viewers. Make sure that joint bars on the gauge side (inside) of the rail clear wheel flanges. You can go a step further and use a razor saw to add a simulated joint, using the blade to just notch the head of the rail. Many modelers save fine details like this for primary scenes and those that are closest to viewers.

Few things more quickly improve the realistic appearance of a layout more than giving ties and rails a coat of paint and some weathering. Nickel-silver rail looks nothing like prototype steel rail, and shiny plastic ties—even if they're molded in brown or black—

This Walthers code 83 HO track was enhanced with Details West joint bars, then painted a variety of rust colors using a brush. The ties were also painted, using a mix of flat dark gray, brown, and grimy black. *Jeff Wilson*

don't appear realistic. Many colors work well, from medium to dark brown, as well as black and grimy black. Be sure to use flat (not glossy) paints.

A good basic approach is to use an airbrush or spray paint to give track a coat of flat dark brown before installing it. Use paint markers or a brush to highlight areas of rail in varied shades of brown and black; ties can be shades of gray, brown, and black. Finish by using an abrasive track-cleaning block to clean paint from the rail heads (which will give them a realistic shine as well).

and heavier the traffic, the larger the plate. Along with alignment, the job of the tie plate is to spread the weight of the rail and load over a broader area, reducing wear.

Plates are either single-shoulder (with one alignment ridge, used on the outside of the rail) or double-shoulder (ridges on both sides of the rail). They generally have four square punched holes for spikes, two on either side of the rail. Most larger plates have four additional holes outside the shoulders to anchor the plate to the tie.

Single-shoulder, four-hole plates are generally used on light rail (100 pounds or less); double-shoulder, eight-hole plates are used for heavier rail and on all high-traffic lines.

Cut spikes are standard in North America for securing rails to wood ties. These have a square shaft with a chisel-shaped tip, and are driven into place with a spike maul or mechanical hammer. The square shaft resists twisting, aiding stability, and the angle of the head clamps the base of the rail, keeping it firmly in place and in gauge.

Even though each tie plate has four spike holes, on most trackage only one is used on each side of the rail. Additional spikes are sometimes used on curves where a lot of lateral thrust (centrifugal force) would tend to broaden the gauge. Standard spike placement is to have spikes staggered on opposite sides of each rail.

Screw spikes have a bolt-style head and threaded shank. They are most often used to secure tie plates to ties and switch stands to headblocks, but are sometimes used to secure the rails as well. They are installed with power wrenches into pre-bored holes in the tie.

Spring clips of various designs are sometimes used to secure rails. On wood ties, this is more common in Europe; concrete ties use clips as well. Clips (and additional braces) are often used in special trackwork on wood ties, such as crossings and turnouts (more on those in Chapter 3).

Rail anchors are used on most mainline tracks. These are C-shaped metal pieces that wrap around the underside of the base of the rail, and

Panel track is prototype railroads' answer to model railroad sectional track. First used in the early 1960s, its primary purpose is for temporary track arrangements (during track repair or when main track is washed out or damaged by a derailment). It's sometimes used to speed construction of spurs and secondary track. *Gordon Odegard*

they are anchored firmly to the rail on either side of a tie. Their purpose is to keep rail from "creeping," which is longitudinal movement that can be caused by train movement of various types (such as by braking forces on downhill grades). Some lines have anchors at every tie; others have them every other tie. It's a feature rarely modeled.

Joint bars are steel members bolted to the web of each rail at each end-to-end joint. A joint bar is used on both sides of the rail, with bolts passing through the joint bars and rail web to secure them. They are made in many sizes to match specific rail profiles. Most are 24" long with four bolt holes, with 36"-long, six-bolt versions on some high-traffic lines. Joints are staggered between rails.

Many joint bar designs have been used, with the goal of reducing stress and torque on the rail while providing support, whether the joint occurs directly above a tie or not.

Compromise joint bars are used to join rail of different sizes, such as where an industrial spur with light rail meets a main line with heavy rail. Compromise bars have a distinctive

stepped profile that allows the top and gauge side of each railhead to match.

Some rail joints must be insulated to separate signal circuits. These have insulating pads between the joint bar and rail web, insulated linings in the bolt holes, and an insulating pad between the butted rail ends. They are often painted white or orange as an indicator.

Support

The track structure, of course, is just the first part of the railroad right of way. Integral to rails and ties is the support for the track: the ballast, roadbed, and subroadbed. Turn the page and we'll examine how these elements work together to allow the right of way to provide a smooth path for trains while negotiating various types of terrain.

CHAPTER TWO

Ballast and subroadbed

A freight rolls westbound behind a 2-8-2 Mikado on Baltimore & Ohio's double-track main line across Indiana in the early 1950s. The right of way features nicely manicured gray ballast atop cinder sub-ballast. The roadbed is neatly defined, and the jointed rail track is well-maintained.
Linn H. Westcott

Track requires a level, stable, resilient base to support it. This base must allow the track structure to flex slightly under load, but be firm enough to avoid deflections that would impede operations or lead to dangerous conditions. It also must provide for proper drainage to avoid erosion and instability.

The subgrade shoulder and slope are clearly visible on the Western Maryland's main line between Hagerstown and Cumberland, Md., in the 1950s. The stone ballast rests directly on the subgrade, with no sub-ballast. *Western Maryland*

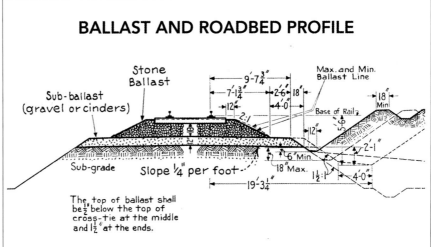

This profile is typical for a high-traffic line. Not all railroads used sub-ballast between the subgrade and ballast. Ballast depth (18" below ties shown here) varied by traffic level and line importance. *Pennsylvania Railroad*

The track, roadbed, and subroadbed together are known as the roadway. Several layers comprise this roadbed and subroadbed. At the top is crushed-rock roadbed, called ballast, that holds the track (it may rest on a finer layer of crushed rock or cinders, called sub-ballast). The roadbed rests atop a base called the subgrade or subroadbed, usually graded, hard-packed earth smoothed to a level profile, but with a crown in the middle to provide drainage. The subroadbed may be shallow or tall depending upon surrounding terrain, with sloped fill material bringing it up to roadbed level. Ditches on either side help form the overall roadbed profile, further allowing drainage.

The drawing above shows a high-traffic mainline profile, as specified by the Pennsylvania Railroad in the 1940s. The profile is typical, but the mechanical departments of individual railroads generally publish their own profile requirements and specifications for different types of track, which vary.

The roadbed and subroadbed accomplish several things. The roadbed supports the weight of the track structure and distributes its weight more evenly across the subroadbed. It locks ties into position, keeping them from shifting, but it also allows the track to flex, allows it to be easily adjusted and realigned if needed, and protects track from frost heaves and other shifts in the surrounding ground. It also resists vegetation growth.

The ballast, sub-ballast, and subgrade together raise the track above the grade of the surrounding land, providing drainage.

Ballast

Crushed rock has long been the most-common ballast material—often quartzite, granite, or limestone—sized to about 1.5"-3.5" for individual rocks. Another material that's still used is crushed steel slag, a byproduct of the steel-making process. The keys are that it be hard enough to resist breaking or abrasion and have sharp edges that lock together well when tamped and distributed around the crossties.

In the 1800s—and on some lines, well into the 1900s—cinders were widely used for both ballast and sub-ballast. They were readily available, inexpensive, and although much smaller than crushed rock, held their shape and still allowed drainage. Cinders can still be found as roadbed on some branch lines and older industrial spurs.

The difference in ballast between the main line and passing siding—tall stone on the main, low cinders on the siding—is apparent on the Illinois Central Gulf near Litchfield, Ill., in 1971. *J. David Ingles*

Workers dump ballast between and along the rails at Union Pacific's Hinkle, Ore., yard in 1950. A tamper will later be used to level and elevate the track. *Union Pacific*

Automated rail maintenance in 1955 included, from foreground, a spike puller, track raiser, tie remover, tie inserter, compressor for spike hammers, ballast distributor, and ballast tamper. *Erie Railroad*

Track was sometimes laid directly on the roadbed, with no ballast. Into the early 1900s this was common for branch lines, yards, and industrial tracks. Over time, these tracks tend to sink into the ground, until at some point all that's visible are the rails (and they're often obscured by grass and other overgrowth). The increasing weight of cars into the early diesel era made this impractical, as too much maintenance was required to keep unballasted track in usable condition.

The use of various types of rock and other material means prototype ballast varies widely in color, with individual railroads often identifiable by the color of their ballast. An example is the "pink lady" quartzite ballast long used by the Chicago & North Western, which comes from a pit in Wisconsin. A key is that rarely are all rocks the same color—the shade often varies among individual stones, accentuating the texture as well as color.

The depth of ballast varies by era and by the amount and type of traffic carried. Class 4 and 5 track (more on

The ballast shaper was the final step after tamping, leaving a well-defined roadbed and profile in its wake. *Erie Railroad*

track classification in a bit)—heavy-haul, high-speed main lines—calls for 12" to 18" of ballast between the bottom of the ties and the subgrade. This creates a distinctive, tall profile. Secondary lines and passing sidings generally have 6"-10" of ballast.

Prototype railroads maintain their ballast continually, especially on main lines and other heavily used track.

With the passage of hundreds of heavy trains, the ballast tends to settle, break down, and lose its profile. It becomes contaminated with fragments of itself (from crushing due to track movement), with surrounding soil, and other impurities such as traction sand and spilled material from loads.

If not maintained regularly—especially on secondary tracks with

 MODELING TIP

Ballast colors and texture

Prototype ballast comes in a wide range of colors, including shades of white, gray, pink, brown, and black. Individual pieces of ballast vary in color—sometimes subtly, and sometimes widely. Check prototype photos and information if you're modeling a specific railroad or region, as ballast color can be a key identifying element for a prototype railroad. Model ballast is available in a wide range of colors and sizes from Arizona Rock & Mineral, JTT Scenery Products, Scenic Express, Woodland Scenics, and others. If in doubt, stick to fine sizes/grades for HO and N scales, with medium for O and S scales. Beware of model ballast that is all the same color and shade—mixing two or more colors can provide a very realistic appearance.

Follow prototype guides in applying ballast to reflect the type of railroad you're modeling. Some prototype lines are beautifully manicured, with sharp ballast and roadbed profiles. Others are more sloppy, with lower ballast profiles, ballast over the ties, and vegetation growing in the roadbed. Sidings and spur tracks often have a lower ballast profile and different ballast type: cinders instead of crushed rock, for example.

This interlocking on Bill Darnaby's HO Maumee Route features tall, nicely maintained ballast on the busy New York Central main line, with lower-profile cinder roadbed under the undulating secondary track at left (note also the smaller rail). These details aptly inform viewers of each track's relative importance. *Bill Darnaby*

A Jordan spreader cuts a fresh ditch profile along the Southern Railway's Carolina & Northwestern High Point to Asheboro, N.C., line in 1987. *Mike Small*

low ballast levels—ties eventually settle down to the subroadbed itself. This creates a situation where passing trains cause ties to sink into the earth, then return. This creates a pumping effect that—especially in wet conditions—siphons soil upward, further contaminating the roadbed and creating unstable track.

To combat this, railroads use a variety of mechanical devices. Tampers travel along the track, elevating it while redistributing the ballast under and between the ties while leveling the track (when needed, new ballast is dumped directly atop the track prior to tamping). Ballast cleaners take that a step further by pulling out ballast, cleaning it, and redistributing the ballast behind it, restoring its profile.

Subroadbed and fills

The subroadbed (subgrade) is earth fill, graded and packed to support the roadbed and track. In some cases the ground itself is simply graded to prep for the track and roadbed—think 1800s low-budget line, or a short spur to an industrial area. In most cases,

the subroadbed is elevated above the surrounding terrain, if only by a couple of feet, to provide for drainage and to ensure that track is level.

Unlike roads, which can usually follow the terrain and deal with grades of 6 percent (and steeper on residential or secondary routes), railroad grades must be kept reasonably level, usually no more than 1 to 1.5 percent if possible (more on grades in a bit).

This means railroad grades are often taller than neighboring street and road grades (often creating situations where streets and roads rise to meet railroads at crossings, creating potentially hazardous conditions—see Chapter 7 for examples).

Although the right of way itself is generally 100 or 200 feet wide, the actual base for the roadbed is generally a minimum of 20 feet wide for a single-track line (measured from shoulder edge to shoulder edge of the subroadbed) and 34 feet wide for double track (the profile drawing on page 19 specified 24 feet for single track and 38 for double on the Pennsy).

Ideally, an 18"- to 30"-wide shoulder of the subroadbed should be visible outside of the edge (toe) of the ballast slope. The subroadbed slopes outward from the shoulder, generally at a 1.5:1 pitch (horizontal to vertical). Well-maintained lines show this, although the shoulder will wear down over time if not re-graded and reshaped regularly, so it may not be apparent on secondary and branch lines.

Although it can't be seen under the ballast, the top surface of the subroadbed is crowned slightly (about 3" at the middle) to encourage proper drainage.

Cuts and retaining walls

A "cut" is the opposite of a fill, where a path for the roadbed must be excavated from a hill or rise in the terrain. The cut must be wide enough to provide the necessary width of the top of the subroadbed, plus room for appropriate ditches along either side. The longer the cut, the larger the ditches must be to carry away water from rain (and snow melt)—especially if the

Railroads use a combination of cuts and fills to keep a level profile through surrounding terrain. The Western Maryland had to excavate a cut (in the distance), then used the earth from the cut to form a fill (under the crossover turnouts). This is at Frostburg, Md., in 1947. *Charles A. Elston*

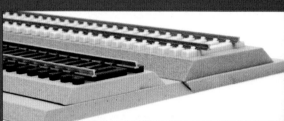

Here's an example of how to vary roadbed height for a siding (left) and main track in HO scale, using Flexxbed roadbed (from Hobby Innovations). The siding is HO scale Atlas track on 3/16" roadbed and the main is Atlas flex with concrete ties on ¼" roadbed; both are atop 3/16" subroadbed. *Jeff Wilson*

Roadbed depth and profile

Varying the height of roadbed and subroadbed is a great way to simulate various ballast profiles and define differences among mainline, secondary, siding, branch line, and spur tracks. Modelers in HO can use combinations of N and HO cork or other commercial roadbed for both roadbed and subroadbed; sheets of cardstock, matboard or styrene can be used to adjust roadbed height in any scale. These materials are also handy for ramping roadbed up to the level of neighboring tracks (it's a good idea to keep model turnouts level). Industrial tracks and spurs can ramp down to the layout surface level. You can see this in practice in the photo on Bill Darnaby's layout (see "Ballast colors and texture" on page 21).

The Northern Pacific built a long, tall fill as a bridge approach on its main line at Logan, Mont. Here a matched set of Fs roll a freight off the bridge onto the fill in 1966. *J.W. Swanberg*

Cribbed retaining walls can have timber or concrete members, with alternating members running lengthwise as well as perpendicular into the earth behind the wall. The wall rises at an angle at a highway overpass along the Western Pacific near Greenville, Calif., in 1947. *Fred Matthews, Jr.*

surrounding slopes are tall. The slopes of the cut are also kept to a 1.5:1 angle to minimize problems with sliding earth and rocks. Narrow cuts can cause problems in the winter, especially in the Midwest and West where blowing snow can quickly fill a cut.

Whenever possible, the earth removed from a cut is used as fill nearby, to avoid having to transport fill long distances. Fill is often needed on either side of a cut where the terrain features rolling hills or mountain foothills.

If it's not possible to keep the slope angle at a proper ratio, a retaining wall is used to hold back the earth. Retaining walls can be made of many materials, including horizontal wood timbers, vertical wood posts (piles), stone, or concrete (the most common material for modern installations). There's a lot more to a retaining wall than is visible: They have significant footings, and are often cribbed, with extensions behind them into the ground.

Retaining walls are generally kept as low as possible. Often a wall 4 or 6 feet tall is sufficient to keep a neighboring slope in check. Retaining walls are rarely taller than 12 to 14 feet, as the forces involved in holding back fill with taller walls becomes significant. Retaining walls are often angled, starting near ground level and elevating

upward—to reach a bridge abutment or tunnel portal, for example.

Retaining walls are often found along tracks in urban areas, where space is at a premium and railroads share space on multiple levels with streets and other railroads. Railroads can be found in cuts below street level, or be elevated above street level. Again, walls should be no taller than absolutely necessary.

In rural areas, cuts are often made through rocky soil (or, in many mountainous areas, through solid rock). These rock faces can be steeper than earth walls if they're stable, but with steep side walls (or extremely tall hills) there's always the threat of rocks, boulders, and other debris being dislodged and landing on the tracks. Railroads guard against this by using slide-detector fences.

Slide fences are found along many routes in rugged and mountainous territory. They have a series of closely spaced, fine horizontal wires mounted on vertical posts. Each wire is insulated from the other and carries a low-voltage current. If a falling rock breaks a wire, it breaks the circuit and triggers surrounding signals to red, alerting crews of a potential hazard.

Tunnels

If a cut and retaining wall aren't sufficient to provide a path for the railroad, a tunnel must be bored through the hill or mountain. Excavating a tunnel is the most expensive way to create a right of way, especially if rock is involved. Tunnels present many operational, safety, and clearance challenges, so railroads will first explore all other options.

Tunnels were reserved for main lines that see heavy traffic. Remember this when placing tunnels on a model railroad: If, in looking at a modeled scene, it's obvious that it's not really needed, the visual effect will be lost.

How a tunnel is built depends on the material encountered and its stability. Lining is required for all but solid rock; this was done with timbers in the 1800s, but progressed to brick, stone, and then concrete by the 1900s.

Railroads will continue cuts with

retaining walls as far as possible before starting a tunnel. The tunnel entrance itself (the portal) is often part of the surrounding retaining walls used on the tunnel approach. Timber construction in the 1800s wasn't long lasting, and was subject to fire. Wood gave way to cut stone and concrete by the 1900s. Vertical side walls with arched tops are most common in North America. Portals often carry the year of their construction on the outside, engraved into the stone or concrete.

Smoke in tunnels was a major problem for railroads, especially

Mid-height retaining walls of stone (left) and concrete (right) hold back fill on either side of Conrail's line at Palmer, Mass., in 1993. *Jeff Wilson*

A northbound Monon freight rolls down the middle of Fifth Street in Lafayette, Ind., in 1967. Timbers line the rails in the concrete surface. Street running presented maintenance and operational headaches for prototype railroads.
J. David Ingles

Industrial trackage in streets often features sharp curves and complex trackwork. This is Conrail's former Pennsylvania Railroad line in Fell's Point (Baltimore), Md., in the 1970s. Note the girder rail and brick surface patched in many places with asphalt.
TRAINS magazine collection

Street trackage

Railroads sometimes share a right-of-way with streets in urban areas. Although this was relatively common into the early 1900s, railroads eventually re-routed most of these tracks because of the many safety and operational challenges in dealing with vehicular traffic, especially on busy lines. Street trackage also presents significant maintenance challenges, namely the inaccessibility to ties and rail hardware and the tendency of track motion to crack and deform the paving material.

Tracks could be found in just about any paving material. Bricks were common into the early 1900s, with asphalt and concrete most common after that. As with railroad crossings, tracks generally have guardrails inside the running rails to ensure a clear flangeway. Some street trackage was laid with girder rail, which has a built-in flangeway as part of the rail (although this was more common for streetcars and interurban lines). Wood timbers often lined the rails to allow the track to flex up and down without damaging the pavement.

Street trackage falls into two main categories: main lines

and industrial tracks. Main lines often traveled down a town's main street. Urban areas often featured industrial tracks that traversed side streets—of varying lengths, from a half a block to several blocks—to get to one or more businesses. Turnouts in pavement require throw mechanisms that can be under ground level, usually with a hinged metal cover protecting it.

With street trackage, train movements are slow-speed operations. Traffic lights on major streets are synched to train operations, allowing trains to proceed directly through without stopping. On branch and industrial lines where switching moves are performed, street tracks are often worked at night, when there's the lowest level of vehicle traffic.

When street tracks are taken out of service, the rails themselves sometimes remain in place. This can be an eye-catching detail to add, as sometimes these rails remain in the pavement for years (sometimes decades) after being abandoned.

Urban areas often have retaining walls of varying heights, with railroads and streets in close proximity. Here a Chicago & North Western transfer pulls a load of auto racks from the railroad's East St. Paul (Minn.) Yard in June 1967. *J. David Ingles*

Slide-detector fences have multiple horizontal electric wires. If falling rock breaks a wire, it sets neighboring signals to red, alerting crews of potential hazards. This is on the Southern Pacific near Hafed, Nev., in 1944. *Union Switch & Signal*

through the steam era. Railroads used a variety of fan and exhaust systems to combat this, sometimes involving doors at the tunnel portals or vertical shafts that allowed smoke to be exhausted upward out of the tunnel.

The structures that held the exhaust equipment were located at one of the tunnel portals. They vary in appearance, but generally look like industrial structures of whatever era they were built.

Multi-track tunnels exist, but are extremely rare because of the expense involved. Double-track areas will begin and end outside of the tunnel entrance.

As with other track, there were ditches next to the roadbed through tunnels to allow for drainage.

Culverts and ditches

Ask any civil engineer what the three most important factors are when designing a highway or railroad grade and the answer will likely be "drainage, drainage, and drainage." Although it's a cliche among those who do this for a living, the exaggeration makes a key point: Nothing will undermine and destroy roadbed and subgrade like water that's become trapped and not allowed to escape, or that's risen above its usual banks and flows against the roadbed.

The primary means railroads provide drainage are by keeping the grade high enough to be above casual water that forms during rain and storms, and to provide ditches, culverts, and bridges to allow water to flow away from the subroadbed. Our challenge as modelers is to design our layouts to reflect this, by visualizing what a real railroad would do in the setting that we're modeling.

The illustration on page 19 shows standards for ditches along rights of way. These are generally the minimum required; lines in areas that see heavy rains, spring snow melt, and other water runoff will require larger ditches. Obviously some prototype lines are extremely well maintained, with well-defined ditches and roadbed slopes, while others have varying levels of maintenance.

One method railroads use to restore and clean up ditches and slopes is with a Jordan spreader. Although often used as snowplows, these machines have adjustable wing blades that can be positioned to the side and well below track level, allowing them to cut new ditches or reshape roadbed as needed.

Culverts are vital elements in railroads' efforts to provide drainage. They're easy to overlook, but culverts are everywhere on railroads, with an estimated 600,000 in place across the U.S. They provide the simple—yet vital—duty of allowing water to flow from one side of an elevated grade to another.

Many culverts are quite small—2 to 4 feet in diameter—and they have been made in a variety of materials, with concrete and corrugated steel the most common in use today. You'll find them at the base of subroadbed grades along most stretches of rights of way—use prototype photos as guides in modeling.

The next step up from a culvert is a small pile trestle or beam bridge. Bridge construction and use is beyond

Tunnels cut from solid rock don't require constructing separate portals. This is on Canadian National in the Canadian Rockies in Alberta. *William A. Akin*

MODELING TIP

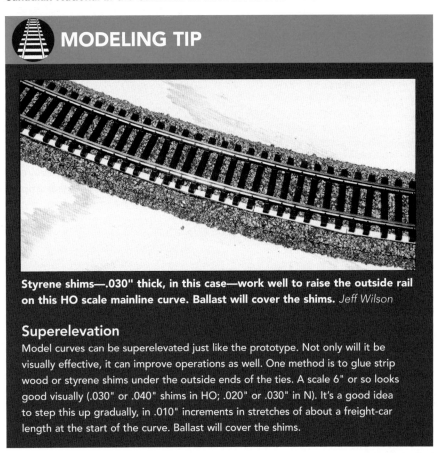

Styrene shims—.030" thick, in this case—work well to raise the outside rail on this HO scale mainline curve. Ballast will cover the shims. *Jeff Wilson*

Superelevation

Model curves can be superelevated just like the prototype. Not only will it be visually effective, it can improve operations as well. One method is to glue strip wood or styrene shims under the outside ends of the ties. A scale 6" or so looks good visually (.030" or .040" shims in HO; .020" or .030" in N). It's a good idea to step this up gradually, in .010" increments in stretches of about a freight-car length at the start of the curve. Ballast will cover the shims.

the scope of this book, but take a look at *The Model Railroader's Guide to Bridges and Trestles* (Kalmbach Media, 2021) for details and examples of culverts, bridges, and trestles of many types.

Curves, superelevation, and grades

Railroads love straight (tangent) track. Since tangent track provides the least

amount of rolling resistance to wheels, railroads work hard to avoid curves whenever possible and minimize them when they're needed. Curved track causes rolling resistance, requires more power/energy to traverse (especially on grades), and increases wear on equipment (rails and rail fasteners as well as wheels). Curves limit train speeds and can result in restrictions to the size and weight of locomotives and

Tunnels in areas where surrounding soil is soft were easier to bore, but require portals, retaining walls, and lining. This is the cut-stone portal and retaining walls at Southern Pacific tunnel 23 near Applegate, Calif. *Ed Anderson; Historic American Engineering Record*

Culverts are vital for providing drainage along rights of way. They can be found in many sizes along the base of railroad subgrades. This one is concrete; others are iron, stone, clay, and timber. *Gordon Odegard*

other equipment. If a curve is needed, a railroad will make it as broad and short as is practical.

Model railroaders are used to measuring curves by their radius in inches, but prototype railroads measure curves by degrees—see the illustration at right—based on the degree of the angle of the curve measured over a 100-foot chord. The higher the measurement in degrees, the sharper the curve. The chart on page 30 shows model railroad equivalents to various prototype measurements.

Curves on prototype railroads are significantly broader than those that we model. A 10-degree curve is considered sharp on a real railroad (574-foot radius). However, scaling this down to a model railroad would mean a 79" radius in HO or 43" in N scale, which would be considered extremely broad on a layout. As a comparison, the Burlington Northern Santa Fe specifies a maximum curve of 7 degrees, 30 minutes (764-foot radius) for new loop-track industrial loading facilities. The curve, still tight by prototype standards but acceptable for slow-speed operation, scales to a 105" radius in HO, which is extremely broad for a model.

To make operation on curves as smooth as possible, prototype railroads often superelevate curves, especially on mainline and high-speed trackage. This is done by raising the outer rail to 3", 4", or 5" above the inner rail (think of

it like a banked curve on a racetrack). Superelevation counteracts centrifugal forces, resulting in a more stable ride at speed while lessening wearing forces on the track.

However, although tall superelevation allows higher speeds by faster trains, it can cause operational and mechanical issues with slower trains, as slow-speed operation results in excessive drag and unbalanced loads that lean toward the bottom rail, resulting in more wear and stress on the lower rail.

The amount of superelevation

depends upon train speeds, and railroads use complex formulas to compute the ideal amount of superelevation. Where all trains will be operating at the same speed, higher superelevation can be used; where trains of widely differing speeds operate, lower superelevation is needed. Using 3", for example, allows higher speed limits and smoother operation for faster trains (passenger trains and fast freights at 70 and 60 mph) but doesn't impede operation of most slower trains (coal drags at 40 or 50 mph).

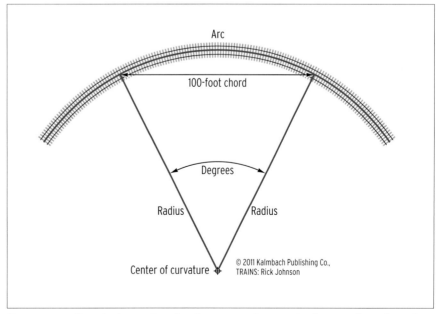

Prototype railroads determine the sharpness of curves in degrees, based on the angle of a triangle formed with a 100-foot chord at the side opposite the angle. *Kalmbach Media*

MODELING TIP

Tunnel construction

To be realistic, a modeled tunnel must look like it belongs—it must look like the modeled line has no choice but to use the tunnel. If there's an obvious path around a hill or mountain, the appearance won't be realistic.

Be sure to provide access to track in tunnels—any tunnel longer than 12" or so will need a method to get inside to clean track, access derailments, and perform any needed maintenance. Avoid turnouts and crossings in hidden track, including tunnels. Make sure track is operating perfectly in a tunnel (and use extra spikes or track nails to secure it) before enclosing a tunnel. Modeled tunnels can be a good way to disguise entrances to staging track through a backdrop or wall.

An eastbound freight heads toward Tunnel No. 1 on Eric Brooman's HO Utah Belt. The rugged territory and steep rock walls give the impression that the tunnel is definitely needed to keep the right of way going forward. *Eric Brooman*

The effect is relatively easy to model. See Superelevation on page 27.

Grades

Whether on prototype railroads or model railroads, grades are measured in the same manner, by percentage based on the amount of rise divided by the amount of run. For example, on a prototype railroad, if a track rises 1 foot vertically over 100 feet of track distance, the grade is 1 percent (1÷100=.01, or 1 percent). The unit of measure doesn't matter; on a model railroad, measuring in inches, a rise of 1 inch over 50 inches of run is 2 percent (1÷50=.02).

Grades are an operational challenge for prototype railroads, as they mean trains carry reduced tonnage and/or operate at lower speeds—a sustained quarter-percent grade can cut the amount of tonnage a locomotive can pull by half. Like curves, railroads do just about anything possible to minimize grades. Grades cause problems both ways, with trains requiring heavy braking to maintain slow, safe speeds when descending long slopes. Grades reduce operating speeds, require much more fuel usage, present operational dangers, increase maintenance to cars and track, and can become bottlenecks on a main line.

How steep is steep? On prototype main lines, grades steeper than 1 percent are rare. Even in mountainous territory, railroads try to keep grades at 2 percent or under. Model railroads can often get away with steeper grades since our trains are much shorter and lighter in comparison, but even then, grades steeper than 2 percent can limit operations.

It's not just long, sustained mountain grades that present problems, however. An otherwise level rail line that follows the undulations of rolling farmland, for example, might have a series of up and down grades each a couple of thousand feet long and no more than a half a percent, but with long trains this will cause slack to continually run in and out as part of the train is going down while another is going up. This can damage couplers and loads, and makes it a challenge to maintain consistent speeds.

Profiles like this are most often found on branch lines and secondary lines, where short trains and slow speeds mitigate their effects. On high-traffic routes, most railroads invested in the cost of smoothing profiles, in some cases re-routing original lines to cut down on grades or curves.

A route's "ruling grade" is the limiting grade found on a particular line (usually a subdivision or other operating district), and is used to determine the maximum load that can be pulled (by a specific locomotive in steam days; in tons per horsepower in the diesel era). The ruling grade is not necessarily the steepest: a shorter, steeper grade may be more easily surmounted than a longer, not-as-steep grade.

Track curvature: Prototype vs. model

Because of space limitations, curved track on model railroads scales out much sharper than prototype track. Prototype track is measured in degrees—the chart at right shows what this means in terms of radius in feet, and how it compares (in inches) in HO and N scales:

Degree	Radius in feet	HO (inches) (Prototype) equivalent	N (inches) (Prototype) equivalent
1	5,730	789"	429"
4	1,433	197"	107"
8	716	99"	54"
12	478	66"	36"
16	359	49"	26"
20	288	40"	22"

Missouri Pacific F units lean into a superelevated curve with their westbound train as they climb Kirkwood Hill in suburban St. Louis in 1964. The outside rail of each track is elevated. Note also the groomed shoulder of the subgrade outside of the ballast profile. *R.R. Wallin*

 **MODELING TIP**

Paul Dolkos added the simple culvert at left to his HO layout by gluing a painted pipe in a hole in the side of the subroadbed and adding scenery. The box culvert at right is stripwood, painted to resemble concrete. *Paul Dolkos*

Culverts

Culverts can easily be added to many scenes, as Paul Dolkos has done here on his HO scale layout. Simple pipe culverts can be made from plastic or brass tubing, painted and weathered appropriately to simulate metal or concrete, and added to a hole cut into an embankment. Iowa Scaled Engineering makes simulated corrugated-metal tubing in many sizes. Small concrete slab and arch culverts can be made from sheet styrene or stripwood, painted to simulate concrete and weathered. Commercial versions are made by Walthers Cornerstone, Woodland Scenics, and others.

Grades can be long and sustained, or they can be short as they follow the ups and downs of surrounding terrain, as here on the Union Pacific in Nebraska in 2006. Each presents operational challenges. *Jeff Wilson*

Quality of track and roadbed: Track classifications

Obviously all prototype track is not maintained to the highest standards. As the photos through this chapter show, track ranges from overgrown, weedy, and undulating to smooth, perfectly maintained, well-profiled main lines, with just about anything in between. Duplicating these varying appearances on a model railroad goes a long way toward realism in capturing the "feel" of a specific type of railroad line, whether it is a high-traffic main, a secondary main, or a branch line.

How varying levels of maintenance are measured on prototype railroads is defined by the Federal Railroad Administration (FRA), which publishes specific classifications for prototype track ranging from Class 1 to Class 9 (plus an additional "excepted" category). Each classification has a maximum allowed speed, along with minimum maintenance standards that must be followed. Each railroad determines the class of the track; in addition, railroads must specify each line as "main track" or "other than main track," which affects maintenance and inspection requirements.

Here's a summary of the classifications:

Excepted track: 10 mph freight; passenger service not allowed. (Only allowed by the FRA under narrow guidelines.)

Class 1: 10 mph freight, 15 mph passenger. This classification covers most yard trackage and industrial spurs, along with some branch lines and short lines.

Class 2: 25 mph freight, 30 mph passenger. This includes many branch lines, short lines, and some regional railroads.

Class 3: 40 mph freight, 60 mph passenger. This includes many regional railroads and secondary main lines of Class 1 railroads.

Class 1 track has a 10 mph top speed. Although this line has some fresh ballast, the jointed rail has a lot of ups and downs. This is the Minnesota Prairie Line at Gaylord, Minn., in 2006. *Jeff Wilson*

Secondary and branch lines often have speed limits of 25 mph. They have a significant ballast profile, but not as deep as a high-traffic main line, and the subgrade often isn't as well defined. Here a local rolls along the Baltimore & Ohio branch line near Pleasant Plains, Ill., in 1967. *J. David Ingles*

Class 4: 60 mph freight, 80 mph passenger. Most mainline trackage falls in this category.

Class 5: 80 mph freight, 90 mph passenger. Not as common as class 4; most high-speed passenger and freight routes use this.

Class 6: 110 mph freight, 110 mph passenger. Exclusive to Amtrak's Northeast Corridor (New York-Washington, D.C.).

Classes 7, 8, 9: Also exclusive to certain stretches of the Northeast Corridor; Class 7 allows 125 mph and Class 8 allows 150 mph; the proposed Class 9 allows 200 mph.

The requirements for each class include more-restrictive specifications for allowed deviations in gauge, rail joints, rail profiles, number (and condition) of ties, and devices for higher classes. Higher classes require more frequent inspections. No grade crossings of any kind (rail or highway) are allowed on Class 8 or 9 lines, and grade crossings on Class 7 lines require barrier-style warning devices.

Track can vary on any given line. For example, a main line may be maintained to Class 4 standards, but have passing sidings that are Class 2, with an industrial lead at a town that's Class 1 track.

Follow the prototype

Follow prototype photos and examples

There's very little ballast—just some cinders—lurking under the track of the New York, Ontario & Western in this view near Apex, N.Y., in July 1956. The O&W had become a slow-speed railroad by this point, and would be abandoned a year later. *Jim Shaughnessy*

in modeling the track, roadbed, and subroadbed on a layout. You don't need to specifically define the class of track being modeled, but a viewer should be able to look at your track and be able to determine whether it represents a one-train-a-day branch line, a high-traffic main line, or an overgrown industrial lead.

Now that we've looked at how the prototype manages track and roadbed,

turn the page and we'll take a look at details of two key elements of track: turnouts and crossings.

CHAPTER THREE

Turnouts, switch stands, and crossings

A Wabash freight waits in a siding for a meet at Holliday, Mo., in the 1950s. The siding turnout is manually operated with a high-profile switch stand, including a classic oil lantern switch light above the target. The small boxes on the headblock ties lock the switch electrically and provide information to the signal system on the turnout's alignment. *Wallace W. Abbey*

Turnouts and crossings are key track elements, as they allow trains to follow multiple routes. Their components and moving parts require sturdier construction than conventional track, and they have many related details, including switch stands, switch motors, locks, heaters, and other devices.

On a stub switch, the switch stand moves the approach rails, aligning them end-to-end with a route (the track to the left in this case). A misaligned rail is a serious problem. *Paul H. Schmidt*

The split-point turnout has two moving rails (points), with ends tapered to match the outside (stock) rails. They allowed higher speeds and eliminated the alignment issues of stub switches. *Gordon Odegard*

Turnouts are often featured prominently in model railroad scenes, especially at junctions, with signals at the ends of passing sidings, and in yards. Understanding how prototype turnouts work and how their components relate to modeled versions will help in modeling them more realistically.

Turnout design

Getting trains from one track to another was a challenge on early railroads. The first popular method of doing this was with a "stub switch." These were controlled by moving the butt ends of the approach rails side-to-side to align with rails of either the main or diverging route (see the photo at the top of this page). This was the most common design used through the 1870s.

Stub switches required precise alignment to operate correctly. If the approach rails were off even slightly, the result was rough operation as the wheels hit the joint, or at worst, a derailment. Keeping them in alignment required regular maintenance, as wheels continually battered the rail ends, causing downward rail deflection (especially as equipment became heavier). Summer heat could cause expansion that closed the operating gap and either stuck the rails in one position or didn't allow enough

clearance to move into the other position.

They required slow-speed operation, and new designs rendered them obsolete for most mainline use by the late 1800s. Some could still be found on seldom-used track, including industrial spurs, into the mid-1900s.

The solution was the split (or split-point) turnout. This design, which became standard in the late 1800s, eliminated the moving butt joints, instead using a pair of moving rails

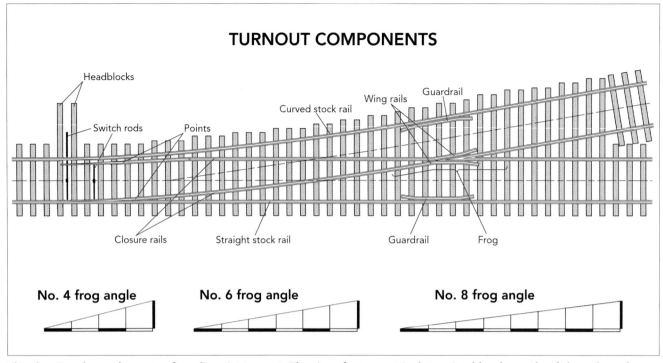

TURNOUT COMPONENTS

Headblocks

Switch rods

Points

Curved stock rail

Wing rails

Guardrail

Closure rails

Straight stock rail

Guardrail

Frog

No. 4 frog angle

No. 6 frog angle

No. 8 frog angle

This drawing shows the parts of a split-point turnout. The size of a turnout is determined by the angle of the rails at the frog, expressed by the length of the run compared to one unit of separation. *Kalmbach Media*

The Union Pacific in 2006 had this mainline turnout leading to an industrial spur. It has an intermediate-height switch stand, manually thrown, with an electric lock that ties to the signal system. Rail braces support the stock rail at the points. *Jeff Wilson*

(points) to guide trains into either route.

The anatomy of a turnout is shown in the drawing above. The stock rails are the solid outside rails that follow the straight and curved (diverging) routes. The frog is where the inner rails from each route meet, forming the point of a "V." The points are the two moving rails that taper at one end to meet the stock rails; the other end of the points ("heels") are joined in a butt joint with the closure rails, which connect the points and frog. The wing rails are extensions of the closure rails that bend to form flangeways on each side of the frog.

Guardrails are used on most prototype turnouts, placed on the inside of the stock rails opposite the frog. They aid in keeping wheel flanges traveling on the proper path through the frog.

Switch rods are located between

(Right) A worker cleans out the area behind a point rail on this turnout, which has a ground throw with a switch lantern on top. The worker's oil can is at right—points need regular lubrication to operate well. *Jack Delano, Library of Congress*

the point rails, keeping them in proper alignment and gauge. The head rod is located between the headblocks (the two long ties where the points meet the stock rails), with the end of the rod extension connecting to either a manual switch stand or powered switch motor. The back rod is located farther inward; it helps distribute the force of the motion of the head rod, and also keeps the points in gauge. Some turnouts have an additional rod or two. (Most model turnouts have a single rod, at the headblocks.)

A note on terminology: The terms "switch" and "turnout" are sometimes used interchangeably, but they have different meanings. On the prototype, the switch refers to the moving parts (points and assemblies)—the part that actually switches the routes—while the turnout is the entire assembly through the frog and diverging tracks.

This low-level ground throw is on an industrial lead track. The large handle at left swings 180 degrees to move the points. You can see how the switch stand is connected to the switch rod. *Jeff Wilson*

MODELING TIP

Choosing switch stands

Operating manual switch stands are available in N and larger scales from Caboose Industries and NJ International. A trade-off in smaller scales is that making a working switch stand that's reliable and durable usually results in a model that's a bit oversize and compromises on realism. The alternative is to use a non-operating switch stand, which are made following many prototypes by Central Valley, Details West, Grandt Line, Micro Engineering, Rapido, Rix, and others, and control the turnout with an electric switch motor or remote manual link.

This HO scale Caboose Industries ground throw works well, but is oversize compared to a prototype switch stand. *Jeff Wilson*

Switch lanterns with built-in round targets were among the most common style found on yard and secondary ground throws from the late steam era through the 1960s. Several manufacturers offered versions of them. *Linn H. Westcott*

The term "facing point" refers to entering a turnout at the point end, where either route can be taken; "trailing point" refers to entering a turnout from either of the diverging routes. Turnouts are directional. When facing the point end, a left-hand turnout has the diverging track going to the left and a right-hand turnout to the right.

Ties used at turnouts ("switch ties") are longer than standard ties to allow room for the diverging track. They're made in lengths from 10 to 16 feet, in 6" increments. The tie layout varies by railroad: some lay ties in a stepped fashion (as in the drawing) with several ties of the same length grouped together, while others use ties in more incremental sizes for a more gradual (less-stepped) appearance.

Two long ties, which straddle the head switch rod, are known as the headblock. This supports the switch

High-level switch stands are used on mainline tracks and other areas where visibility is important. Levers on these stands are moved horizontally across the top of the stand's base. This is on the Indiana Harbor Belt in 1943.
Jack Delano, Library of Congress

Gulf, Mobile & Ohio used semaphore blades as targets on high-level mainline switch stands. The conductor of a gas-electric is at a stand in August 1958. *Paul Larson*

stand or power switch mechanism. The headblock can extend to either side of a turnout, depending upon neighboring obstructions and clearance.

The track structure at turnouts is subjected to more stress than on conventional track. Forces from trains negotiating curves, pounding action from wheels passing through frogs and points, lateral stress on stock rails from forces acting on the points, and the necessity of precise alignment of all components, means that track is more heavily reinforced at turnouts.

Angled rail braces are typically used on the outside of the stock rails at the points and on the outside of other curved rails; other supports include additional braces and support at the frog and extra spikes in tie plates throughout. Construction varies by use:

a turnout on a high-speed mainline crossover will be more substantially built than a turnout on an industrial spur.

Turnout angles

Turnout sizes are indicated by the sharpness of the angle of the diverging track at the frog. Size is measured by number in terms of the number of units of length per one unit of separation at the frog. For example, a turnout that diverges one foot over 10 feet of length is a no. 10 turnout, and so on. In general, broader turnouts allow higher speeds with fewer mechanical issues and restrictions regarding length of cars and locomotives.

As with curves, standards defining "sharp" and "broad" differ greatly

between prototype and model turnouts. Most model railroad turnouts on the market range from no. 4 (considered sharp) to no. 8 (broad). On the prototype, however, even a no. 10 turnout is considered sharp, with speed limited to about 20 mph. High-speed turnouts, used on mainline tracks, are often no. 18 or 20. In addition, some prototype turnouts have extended switch sections, giving them the effect of a broader turnout and allowing higher speeds.

Turnouts can also be placed on curves, although railroads avoid this if possible on mainline tracks. Slow-speed operations (such as in yards and on industrial tracks) will see sharper curves and intricate trackwork, with crossings and turnouts overlapping each other.

Switch stands

A switch stand is a manual device, spiked or bolted to the headblock, that moves the point rails back and forth. Moving a lever on the stand rotates a series of gears and links that pull or push the switch rod, moving the points and holding them in position.

The switch stand can be mounted on either side of any turnout. Clearance is sometimes the determining factor; safety is key, with the location chosen to keep the operator away from neighboring tracks and other safety hazards whenever possible.

A target on a vertical mast rotates to indicate the route selected. This is a signboard (in many shapes), generally showing green for the primary route and red for the diverging route; yard and secondary tracks often use white (main) and yellow (diverging). The target shape usually varies for each route.

Through the early diesel era, switch stands in yards and station areas were illuminated at night by oil lanterns that displayed red or green. By the 1940s, these were replaced in many locations by electric lanterns. Reflectorized colored lenses had been used in many low-traffic and rural locations. By the 1960s, the coming of Scotchlite led to most switch stands receiving reflectorized, colored targets, replacing lights and colored lenses.

Switch stands fall into two broad categories: Low-level (ground throw) stands, with targets 24" or shorter, and high-level (column-throw or vertical-throw) stands, which have intermediate (36" to 48") or tall (up to 7 feet) targets.

Ground throws have handles that lay flat on the headblock parallel to the track. The handle moves in the vertical plane: Lifting it through a 180 degree arc to the other side of the headblock changes the route. Through the 1970s, most of these handles resembled clubs, with long cast arms with notched-squared ends. Modern ground throws typically have a loop at the end, and are designed to be more ergonomically friendly and easier to operate. Ground throws are most often founds in yards

Modern ground throws often have large handle-style levers. *Paul Dolkos*

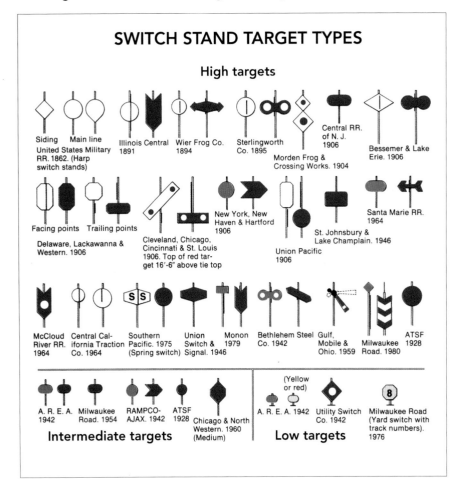

Many styles of switch stand targets have been used. This illustration shows some of the more common ones used through the years. *Kalmbach Media*

Operating switch stand targets

Modeler Bill Darnaby, well known for his HO scale Maumee Route layout, powers his turnouts with under-table switch machines, but uses a simple method to make the targets on his switch stands operable. He mounts the targets on a wire mast, then drills a hole through the base of the switch stand casting to allow the wire to pass through. The switch stand is then secured to the headblock ties. Bending the base of the wire at an angle as shown allows the throw bar to turn the wire when the switch machine lines the turnout.

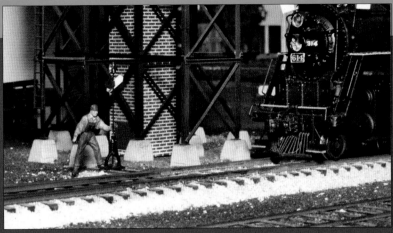

Although the switch stand itself is non-operating, the target turns: it's controlled through movement of the throw bar, which moves the mounting wire attached to the target. Bill Darnaby made the working target on his HO scale Maumee Route layout. *Two photos: Bill Darnaby*

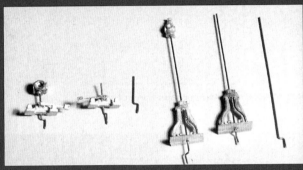

Drill a hole vertically through the switch stand casting. A steel wire holds the target at top; a pair of 90-degree angle bends at the bottom allow the mast to turn. The technique works for high or low stands.

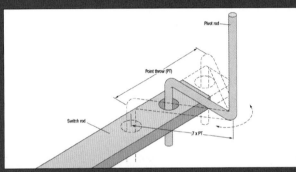

The end of the mast fits in a hole in the throw bar. The length of the horizontal section should be 70 percent of the distance of throw-bar travel.

At mechanical interlocking plants, a system of rods and levers traveled from the tower to turnouts to line them (at left). These turnouts generally did not have targets, with trains relying on the plant's signals for route information. This is at New York Central's Delray Tower (Detroit) in 1966. *J. David Ingles*

Some interlocking plants used air-powered switch machines as part of an electro-pneumatic control system.
Willard V. Anderson

Since the 1940s, electric switch machines have been the standard for turnouts controlled remotely (by dispatcher or interlocking operator). *Gordon Odegard*

Switch heaters have an electric or propane heater, with a blower to direct hot air through ductwork to the switch points. The planks between the rails protect the heat ducts. This is a spring switch on the Santa Fe in the 1980s. *Gordon Odegard*

and industrial tracks where speeds are slow, but can be found on mainline tracks at some locations as well.

With a tall stand, the throwing lever travels in a horizontal plane. The top of the mechanism looks like a small table about 36" tall. The handle, which hangs downward, is hinged to the mechanism at this level; raising the handle allows it to engage the mechanism. It is then rotated, moving the points, and the handle lowered and locked.

High-level stands are used on mainline tracks and wherever increased visibility is desired. Railroads have their own specifications regarding target height, target color, and switch-stand style based on specific installation situations and placement.

Prototype switch stand targets have been made in a tremendous variety of shapes and sizes. The chart on page 40 shows some that have been popular over the years. Target shapes were once unique to manufacturers, but later adopted by individual railroads as standard. Some modern targets include arrows showing which direction the turnout is routed.

Manual switch stands are secured with padlocks to prevent unauthorized use. As an additional measure of safety, manually controlled turnouts located on main lines usually have electrically powered locks as well. Look for a circuit controller mounted at or next to the headblock and throw mechanism. These devices allow remote locking/ unlocking (by the dispatcher) and on signaled lines include contacts that are tied to the block signal system. This will set neighboring signals to red if the turnout is opened (or left open).

Switch machines and powered devices

Remotely operated switches began appearing at interlocking plants in the late 1800s. Turnouts were initially controlled mechanically, by levers that

Spring switches have sprung points, allowing trailing-point movements from either route entering the turnout. They are indicated by an "S" or "SS" on the target, or by a separate sign. *TRAINS magazine collection*

Three-way turnouts have two sets of points to direct trains to one of three routes. They're common in terminals and industrial areas where space is tight. *Alex L.H. Darragh*

extended from the interlocking tower and then through systems of rods and levers to the turnout. Each turnout generally had two levers going to it: One to line the switch and one to lock the points. Although mechanical interlocking plants began declining in number by the 1950s, some remained in service through the century.

By the early 1900s, most new interlocking plants used either electro-pneumatic (machines powered by compressed air, controlled electrically) or straight electrical control for lining switches. The machines that did this were distinctive, and had a large, boxy assembly located atop and adjacent to the headblocks. The shape and design of pneumatic and electric switch machines varied by builder and era; Union Switch & Signal and General Railway Signal were the two main suppliers.

The advent of Centralized Traffic Control in the 1930s led to remote (dispatcher) control of long lengths of mainline track, with electrically powered turnouts tied to signals in many locations: namely the ends of passing sidings, mainline crossovers, and junctions.

These switch machines generally don't have separate targets indicating route selection. Instead, they rely on the adjoining signals to indicate to trains the route (and speed) they are to take. As Chapters 4 and 5 show, these locations have other details, including neighboring equipment cases, cables tied to communication lines, and signals.

Another device found at remotely operated turnouts is a switch heater. Winter weather can impede switch operation, as points can become frozen in place or become jammed from ice

forming in (or pieces of ice falling in) gaps between the points and stock rail. A switch heater rests next to the turnout and directs hot air to the point rails through the ductwork, melting any snow and ice and keeping it from building up. These can be powered by electricity or propane (propane heaters will have a common horizontal propane tank nearby). Switch heaters are common across the northern states and Canada.

Special turnouts

Turnouts come in many variations. For high-speed operations, namely at crossovers on double-track main lines, railroads use closing-frog turnouts. On these, the closure rails at the wing move to contact the frog, eliminating the gap of the other route's flangeway. This eliminates the shock of the wheel hitting the gap and also eliminates the

Double-slip switches serve as both a shallow-angle crossing and a turnout. They're complex, and usually found only in tight spaces such as passenger terminals; here, several are located along diagonal tracks passing through a Central of New Jersey yard. *David Plowden*

chance of the wheel flange "picking" the frog and taking the wrong path.

Spring switches allow trailing-point moves on either route without throwing the switch. The points are spring-loaded, so the wheel flanges can push them aside to pass through. Spring switches are most often used at the ends of passing sidings and at the beginning and end of double-track territory, so that trains do not have to stop to re-set the switch after clearing it. They are marked by a sign on the switch stand (usually an "S" or "SS").

Electrical considerations and relative weight of equipment precludes easily modeling spring switches on model railroads, but we can still simulate their locations by adopting the signs for them.

Three-way turnouts have, as the name implies, three routes. They require two switch stands (or switch machines) to control their two sets of points. They are most often used in yards, terminals, and industrial areas where space is tight; they're generally restricted to slow speeds.

A wye turnout has both routes curving (diverging) from the straight path. They're sometimes found at junctions, at the start of double track, or on the tails of wye tracks designed to turn equipment.

Slip switches are a combination of a shallow-angle crossing and turnout. They fall into two categories: single- and double-slip. Single-slip switches allow trains to pass between routes on one side of the crossing; double-slip switches allow changing paths on either route. Slip switches are used where space is at a premium, namely yards (especially large passenger terminals with multiple stub-end lead tracks approaching the terminal).

Slip switches are complex, high-maintenance installations that require slow speeds. Prototype railroads avoid using them unless absolutely necessary.

Crossings

Crossings allow two rail lines to cross without being able to change routes. Rails of the routes meet at four frogs (just like turnouts), with flangeways and guardrails. They are measured by the angle of their crossing, which can be anywhere from 90 degrees to extremely broad. Common sizes of assembled crossings in HO and other scales include 90, 60, 45, 30, 25, and 12.5 degrees.

Railroads minimize crossings whenever possible. They are maintenance-intensive installations: the constant battering of wheels over the rails at the flangeways and frogs takes their toll on track, and crossings often require speed restrictions.

Crossings fall into two broad categories: Those on main tracks and branch lines, which see scheduled traffic; and those along industrial leads and spurs that only see slow-speed movements when cars are being switched. Crossings on main and branch lines need some type of traffic control: a full interlocking system, automatic signals, manual signals, a swinging gate, or a simple stop sign. The type of control will depend upon the amount of traffic on each line. You can see examples of these in Chapters 4 and 8.

(Right) Crossings allow tracks to meet at grade. They are high-maintenance devices, as the frog castings take a beating from wheels at the flangeways. *Michael C. Calhoun*

Trackwork in yards and industrial areas can be quite complex. This 1950s scene on the Missouri Pacific includes curved turnouts, turnouts overlapping, and a crossing through a turnout. This is all slow-speed trackage. *TRAINS magazine collection*

Lineside signals

Signals are a vital link in the safety chain of railroading. Their main purposes are to allow trains to follow each other safely, to warn of opposing trains, and to indicate routes and give permission to enter tracks at interlockings where multiple routes diverge or tracks cross.

A Louisville & Nashville train splits a pair of classic upper-quadrant semaphores on a single-track main line in 1954. The train has a clear (vertical) signal; the semaphore opposing the train is at stop (horizontal). A cable runs from the pole line to the signal at right, while a buried cable runs under the tracks to the signal at left.
William A. Akin

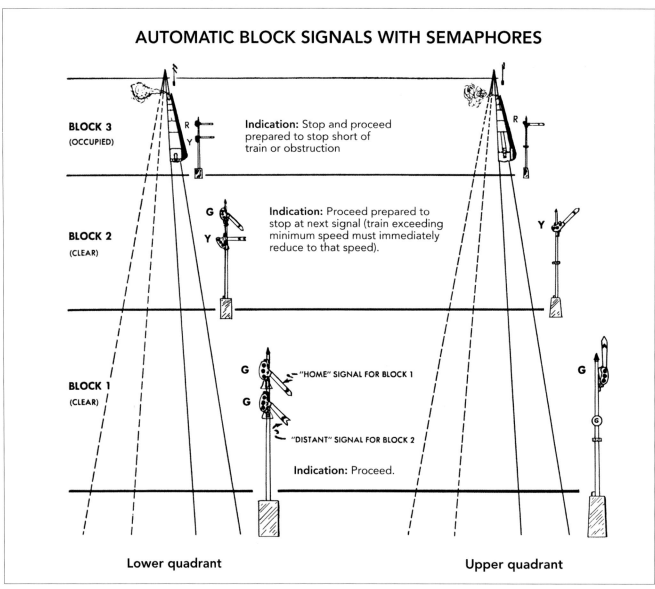

AUTOMATIC BLOCK SIGNALS WITH SEMAPHORES

BLOCK 3 (OCCUPIED)

R
Y

Indication: Stop and proceed prepared to stop short of train or obstruction

BLOCK 2 (CLEAR)

G
Y

Indication: Proceed prepared to stop at next signal (train exceeding minimum speed must immediately reduce to that speed).

Y

BLOCK 1 (CLEAR)

G
G

"HOME" SIGNAL FOR BLOCK 1

"DISTANT" SIGNAL FOR BLOCK 2

Indication: Proceed.

G

G

Lower quadrant

Upper quadrant

Block signals indicate train occupancy. For most systems, red means a train is in the next block, with yellow indicating a train is two blocks ahead. *Kalmbach Media*

History and types of installations

As train frequency and speeds increased in the mid-1800s, getting trains safely around and past each other required more than just timetables and telegraph communications. The result was the adaptation and development of various types of signals to show track occupancy and indicate permission to be on specific blocks or areas of track.

Manually operated signals were first used in England in the 1830s; U.S. railroads followed by the 1850s. Track occupancy circuits were developed by the 1870s, enabling signals to operate automatically in many locations.

Signals at junctions—similar to highway traffic lights at intersections—were being installed as part of interlocked systems by the 1870s.

How each railroad adopted signaling—and the types of signals used by each—varied widely, with most main lines and busy traffic routes having some type of signal system by 1900.

Let's start with a look at the various types of signal installations and how they evolved.

Manual blocks: The earliest signal systems were manual, with operators setting signal indications based on information from a dispatcher or neighboring block operator. The most

common manual block systems used operators at each station to set signals indicating whether trains should stop or proceed. The "block" was the stretch of track between signals (usually between stations), which could be several miles long.

Although manual blocks worked well, operator error was always a possibility, especially as train speeds and the number of trains increased. Manual block systems were also limiting in terms of capacity because of the length of the blocks. These factors meant most busy lines shifted to automatic signals as they became practical from the 1880s into the 1900s.

Operators at interlocking towers controlled signals and turnouts within the interlocking plant, such as this crossing between Erie Lackawanna and Penn Central at North Judson, Ind. Color position-light signals guard the crossing, which is in its last years of operation in 1975. *Ed DeRouin*

A Union Pacific train waits at a red-over-red (stop) signal while a BNSF double-stack train clears the diamonds (crossings) at Rochelle, Ill. The signal bridge carries searchlight signals, controlled by CTC, for both mainline tracks. *Jeff Wilson*

The manual block system, however, remained a practical option for lines with lower levels of traffic. Many secondary lines that saw just a few trains per day remained under manual block control into the 1950s.

The signals used were often the same as train-order boards (more on those in a bit).

Automatic block signals (ABS): By the 1870s, engineers had developed methods of detecting train occupancy by sending low-voltage electricity through the rails. The presence of a train closed a circuit by shunting electricity between the rails. A relay added to the system was then energized, triggering signal indications.

Automatic signals offered several advantages over the manual block system. Blocks could be divided into smaller segments, allowing higher train capacity (1 to 2 mile blocks are common). Signals could then convey the status of not just the upcoming block, but the following block as well. Operators were no longer required to clear signals for trains, eliminating a possible source of human error. By the 1890s, railroads had equipped many high-traffic main lines with ABS; its use would continue growing into the 1900s.

A development of ABS in the early 1900s was "absolute-permissive" block signaling, or APB. With APB, signals also responded to train direction, offering better protection for opposing movements. With APB, a train heading south, for example, passing a signal at a passing siding, would "tumble down" all opposing (northward) signals to red through the location of the next passing siding. Signals behind that train, however, would go to yellow and green as the train cleared, allowing a trailing train to follow the first train at a safe distance.

With ABS or APB, it's important to understand that the signals indicate occupancy, and don't imply permission to be on a specific track. Through the

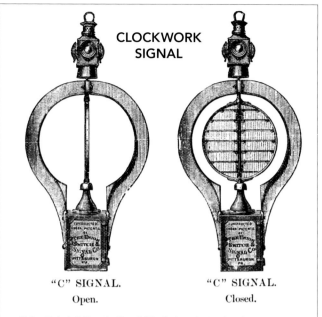

CLOCKWORK SIGNAL

"C" SIGNAL.
Open.

"C" SIGNAL.
Closed.

Union Switch & Signal offered this clockwork signal in the 1870s. The signal at left is in the clear (open) position; the signal at right shows the disk rotated closed. The clockwork mechanism will then slowly rotate the disk back to the open position.

A Soo Line freight is looking at a red-yellow-red (diverging approach) signal, which tells the crew it's taking a siding at restricted speed at Grayslake, Ill. Centralized Traffic Control allows the dispatcher to directly control turnouts and signals to arrange meets between trains. *Jim Hediger*

The operator at Whitefield, N.H., raises a signal ball into position at the Maine Central/Boston & Maine crossing in 1979. Ball signals were common in New England; this one lasted into the 2000s. *Ben Bachman*

1960s, this permission was usually granted through timetables and train orders, and since then, various forms of track warrants issued directly to trains from the dispatcher via radio.

As train speeds increased, zones and levels of protection increased, indicating occupancy two or three blocks ahead instead of one. Many railroads added additional signal indications, usually by blinking lights in green or yellow. Most main lines today are protected by some version of APB signaling.

Centralized Traffic Control (CTC): The ultimate in direct signal and train control by dispatchers is Centralized Traffic Control. It allows the dispatcher to use a control panel

to line turnouts and control signals at remote locations, eliminating the need for train orders and local operators. The first installation was a 40-mile stretch on New York Central in 1927, and CTC greatly grew in popularity and miles operated, first on relatively short portions of line that were operating bottlenecks, but eventually over multiple divisions (Union Pacific completed a 625-mile stretch of CTC on its western main line in 1949).

Most high-traffic main lines are now controlled by CTC. The systems have evolved from early mechanical switches on panels to microprocessor-controlled, screen-based systems.

On CTC lines, the dispatcher does not control all signals. Railroads

use APB block signals between the sidings and junctions controlled by the dispatcher. The specific installations controlled by CTC are usually called "control points," or CPs; they are numbered according to their milepost number.

Interlockings and junctions: Signals are often used to control train movements where tracks cross, at junctions with one or more diverging routes, or at crossovers on double-track main lines. In the mid-1800s these signals were controlled manually on-site by operators who lined turnouts and set signals. This was labor-intensive and subject to human error, especially at complicated junctions with multiple tracks and routes.

In 1870, the first U.S. junction with signals and turnouts that were "interlocked"—mechanically interconnected, ensuring that clearing one route would automatically lock out any other conflicting route—was installed. The interlocking system ensured that an operator couldn't accidentally line turnouts and signals against a route already cleared.

These were controlled by interlocking towers, two-story buildings housing the operator and control panels and levers on the top floor and the mechanisms on the bottom floor (one-story installations were more rare, and were typically called "cabins"). The trackwork within the operator's control is known as the "interlocking plant."

Thousands of interlocking installations were in place by the early 1900s, with an estimated 4,200 plants operating by the mid-1950s. They began dwindling with increased control directly by dispatchers via CTC, and by automatic signal circuits installed at many simple crossings. By the 1990s only a few hundred remained in service; they are now virtually gone from the railroading scene—but their signals remain, controlled remotely by dispatchers.

Signals at interlockings are treated differently than block signals, as they give permission to enter the plant, or enter track on a specific route. To differentiate them from block signals, interlocking signals usually have two or three heads, allowing more indications to show both routing and speed.

Since the early 1900s, there have been two main suppliers of railroad signals. Union Switch & Signal Co. (US&S, purchased by American Standard in 1968; later Ansaldo Signal), and General Railway Signal Co. (GRS, acquired by Alstom Signaling Inc. in 1998). Although both companies have always offered similar products, many details differentiate them. Other companies have also produced signals, most notably the Hall Signal Co., which was acquired by US&S in 1925.

Signal types

Many types of signals have been used by railroads, including ball signals, disk

Hall disc signals (also called "banjo" signals) used a disc that moved inside a clear space in the target, with a separate lens above. This one is on the Reading's Trenton, N.J., branch in 1946. *Charles S. Freed*

The Southern Pacific operated lower-quadrant semaphores longer than any other railroad. Here a freight passes Union Switch & Signal Style B lower-quadrant semaphores in New Mexico in 1987. The top "home" signal shows occupancy in the next block; the lower "distant" signal shows occupancy two blocks ahead. *Alex Mayes*

Signal indications

In some ways railroad signals are like highway traffic signals, but they differ in several important respects. Since the late 1800s the basic colors used are red, yellow, and green, with corresponding semaphore positions at horizontal (red), 45 degrees (yellow), and 90 degrees (green). Each signal aspect has a different meaning. Some are common among all railroads, but many are particular to certain railroads or have their own specific rules (especially at interlockings).

The chart at right shows searchlight signals, but the same rules follow regardless of the type of signal. In signaling, you'll hear three terms: aspect, name, and indication. The aspect is the actual color, or combination of colors shown (or semaphore or light position)—for example, "green." The name is the formal name given to the aspect in that situation ("clear"). The indication is the instruction provided by the signal ("proceed"). These are easy to understand with single-head, three-aspect block signals, but can get complex on busy routes or complex junctions with multi-head signals.

Signals with number plates on the mast below the signal head (or a sign plate with a "P") are "permissive" signals, allowing trains to proceed at restricted speed after stopping at a red aspect. Signals with no number plate are "absolute" signals, requiring trains to stop and stay at a red aspect. Most block signals between junctions and passing sidings are permissive signals, while home signals at junctions and interlockings, as well as signals at passing sidings and other control points, are absolute signals.

The chart shows several common indications as listed in the Consolidated Code of Operating Rules. Be aware that signal use has evolved and rules have changed over the years, and some railroads use additional signal aspects or have variations. Check a rulebook for the railroad (and era) you model for an accurate description.

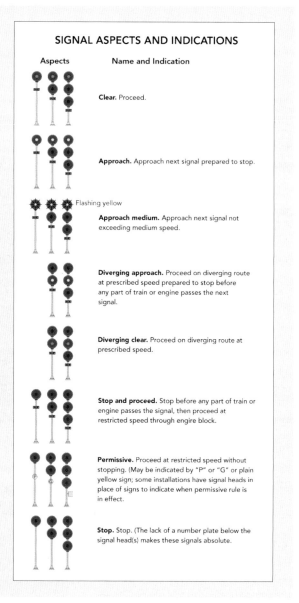

SIGNAL ASPECTS AND INDICATIONS

Aspects — **Name and Indication**

Clear. Proceed.

Approach. Approach next signal prepared to stop.

Flashing yellow

Approach medium. Approach next signal not exceeding medium speed.

Diverging approach. Proceed on diverging route at prescribed speed prepared to stop before any part of train or engine passes the next signal.

Diverging clear. Proceed on diverging route at prescribed speed.

Stop and proceed. Stop before any part of train or engine passes the signal, then proceed at restricted speed through engire block.

Permissive. Proceed at restricted speed without stopping. (May be indicated by "P" or "G" or plain yellow sign; some installations have signal heads in place of signs to indicate when permissive rule is in effect.

Stop. Stop. (The lack of a number plate below the signal head(s) makes these signals absolute.

---

signals, semaphores, color-light signals, searchlight signals, and position-light signals. Some are particular to regions or specific railroads. Many were short-lived in use, but other types remained in service for long periods of time (100 years or more). Because of this, signals can be a great way to lock in a time and place on a model railroad.

Ball signals: The earliest manual signals at junctions were baskets elevated on masts with pulleys. Their position on the mast (high, middle, or low) and color (black or white) conveyed information on train locations or permission to enter track. The baskets soon gave way to large cylinders or spheres, usually red, and eventually acquired the name "ball signal."

The number of balls on a mast varied by installation, depending upon how many indications were needed. The number of balls visible, or raised, indicated which railroad had the right of way (these signals are where the term "highball" comes from). Lanterns were swapped for the balls for nighttime operation.

Ball signals were especially common in New England. Although many were converted to other signal types, some ball signals remained in service at junctions through the late 1900s, with at least one (at Whitefield, N.H.) serving into the 2010s.

Clockwork signals: Among the first automatic signals were those with clockwork mechanisms. A passing train tripped the signal—a rotating disc in a housing—to its closed position via a track circuit relay. A clockwork mechanism then slowly turned the signal 90 degrees to the clear (open) position.

Clockwork signals first appeared in the 1870s, but were obsolete by the 1890s. Although they provided a degree of safety when trains were short and train speeds were slow, they had serious shortcomings in that they didn't accurately report whether a block was occupied—they gave only a rough gauge of when a train had last passed.

Disc signals: Disc signals have a round head with a large clear round opening, and can show two indications.

On early upper-quadrant semaphore signals, the operating mechanism (left, with relays and other electrical gear) was in a cabinet at the base of the mast.

Trains magazine collection

This closeup of the rear of an upper-quadrant semaphore shows the light housing, and how the lenses rotate in front of the light as the blade moves to each position.

Linn H. Westcott

Color-light signals have a separate lens and bulb for each color. Their advantage is that they have no moving parts. This one uses an equipment case as a base. *Gordon Odegard*

Some tri-color signals have lenses grouped in a triangle in a round target. This is on Southern Pacific near Newcastle, Calif. Tunnel 18, a relatively short double-track bore, is in the background. *Ed Anderson; Historic American Engineering Record*

Color-light signals are now replacing many older searchlight signals. Large hoods are common, shading the lenses from direct sunlight. This new CSX installation near Iona Island, N.Y., uses satellite communications. *Scott A. Hartley*

A red disc moves inside the housing to show "stop," and the disc moved out of view to the side to show "clear." A small, round lens at the top echoed the disc indication, and this was illuminated by an oil lantern for nighttime operation.

The disc signal (also known as the "banjo signal" for its shape) was developed by Thomas Hall (of the Hall Signal Co.) in 1869, and it became popular in many areas through the next few decades, with more than 4,000 in service (variations were used as grade-crossing signals as well) by 1900.

They were triggered by track circuitry and used magnets to move the disc, so did not use electric motors. Since they could only provide two indications, some railroads used a pair of signals on a mast, with the top signal the "home" signal, indicating occupancy in the next block; the bottom signal was the "distant" signal, showing occupancy two blocks ahead (usually with a yellow disc instead of red).

Disc signals were obsolete by the 1910s, and most were soon replaced by electrically operated semaphores or

Searchlight signals have a rotating internal mechanism that moves colored lenses in front of a single bulb/reflector. A relay case sits across the track, with a motor-car setout in front of the signal. This is on the Milwaukee Road in 1973.
Gordon Odegard

light signals that could provide three indications. A few survived in service as late as the 1950s.

Lower-quadrant semaphores: The first semaphore signals appeared in the 1860s. Early semaphores were lower-quadrant designs with two aspects: Stop was the arm at horizontal; clear was the blade lowered to a 60-degree angle. To allow for viewing at night, semaphores included glass lenses (red, green, or yellow depending upon specific useage) that rotated in front of a light source as the blade moved. Early lights were oil lanterns, replaced by electric bulbs as they became available.

Because most only allowed two indications, it was common for block signals to use two semaphores on the same mast. As with disc signals discussed earlier, the top signal was the "home" signal and the bottom the "distant" signal. Blade shapes also differed, often with a pointed blade for the home signal and notched blade for the distant signal. Some three-aspect lower-quadrant signals were made, but they were rare (most commonly used for train-order signals—more on those in a bit).

Semaphore blades have a heavy casting that houses the lenses and secures the blade (which is usually wood or thin sheet metal). Early installations were mechanically powered by rod linkage, usually at interlockings. Early block signals were electro-pneumatic or electro-gas, powered by compressed carbonic gas. As electricity became widely available, electric motors proved to be the most reliable and most efficient way of moving blades, and they became standard by the late 1890s. The blades were counter-balanced so that a power failure would rotate them to the "stop" position, making them as fail-safe as possible.

Lower-quadrant signals were used in new installations into the 1910s, and most were replaced by more modern signals by the 1950s. A few, however, lasted in service into the 2000s (notably on some Union Pacific ex-Southern Pacific lines).

Upper-quadrant semaphores:

A Norfolk & Western train approaches a position-light signal giving the equivalent of a red-over-yellow aspect (diverging approach). The Pennsylvania and other railroads it controlled used these signals. *Paul Gibbs*

Erie Lackawanna E units in freight service pass a color position-light signal at Pullman Junction, Ill., in 1972. These signals used color as well as the simulated semaphore placement to provide aspects. *Thomas E. Hoffmann*

The first three-aspect upper-quadrant semaphores were developed by Frank Patenall in 1903, and it was signals from the two main manufacturers—US&S and GRS—in 1908 that popularized the design. The design could better show three aspects: horizontal/red; angled upward at 45 degrees/yellow, and vertical/green. This allowed one signal to replace two-headed lower-quadrant installations. The two most popular were the US&S style S and the GRS Model 2A, and they could be found on railroads across the country.

Early semaphores had their control mechanisms mounted in a cabinet at the base of the mast. By 1912,

Following passage of an eastbound train, this Union Pacific westbound freight gets a yellow aspect on a dwarf searchlight signal, allowing it to move out of the passing siding and back to the main line for its trip through Moffat Tunnel. *Jeff Wilson*

manufacturers were placing the motor at the top of the mast, resulting in a simpler, more reliable mechanism.

Upper-quadrant designs remained popular with some railroads even after other light-only signal types were developed, as the semaphore has redundancy—dual aspects of a signal light plus the visual arm position—especially handy if a bulb fails. They

remained the most-common signal type installed through the 1930s.

The biggest issue with semaphores was that their mechanisms were labor-intensive to maintain, especially as they became older. And, since their moving parts were in the open, they could be fouled by snow and ice. The reliability and lower expense of light-only signals eventually doomed semaphores, and

although few new semaphores were installed after 1940, many remained in service through the 20th century. Some can still be found in 2022, although the few that remain are disappearing quickly.

Railroads used a variety of blade shapes (pointed, squared-end, notched) and colors to indicate their service, with variations indicating a block

Some dwarf semaphore signals were actually rotating disks with a painted semaphore blade and lenses that rotated in front of a bulb. *Jeff Wilson*

This New York Central dwarf semaphore can provide two aspects: red and yellow. *New York Central*

Motor-car signals are low-level targets that display neighboring track block occupancy to maintenance crews aboard track speeders and hi-rail trucks. They generally have two aspects. *Two photos: Gordon Odegard*

signal or an interlocking distant or home signal.

Color-light signals: The color-light signal has a separate bulb for each indication, with each head usually having a red, yellow, and green lamp against a black or dark gray oval target. They began appearing around 1914, when light-bulb technology had advanced enough to produce a long-lasting, bright filament that could easily be seen in daylight. The lenses focus the beam down the track, and shades above each lens help viewing when sunlight is shining on the target (some versions have a single large hood grouped over all the lenses)

The most common arrangement is vertical, with green on top; many railroads opted for triangular-grouped heads as well. Two-light targets were used in some installations (especially at interlockings or on dwarf signals); some modern installations include four or five lights to show additional aspects.

To conserve energy and increase bulb life, color-light signal installations

are often "approach lit." This means that the signals are normally dark, or unlighted, and do not come on until a train is in a neighboring block.

The coming of searchlight signals in the 1920s dropped the popularity of color-light signals through much of the 1900s. However, since the 1990s, new versions of color-light signals have become the most-common signal type, and new installations—using LEDs and updated, efficient technology—are rapidly replacing older searchlight, position-light, and semaphore signals.

Searchlight signals: The searchlight signal was revolutionary when introduced by Hall in 1920. It uses a single lamp (in a round target head) with an internal mechanism that moves one of three colored lenses in front of the lamp. An efficient reflector and highly focused (directional) lens allows a low-wattage bulb to create a bright beam that can be seen up to a mile away with low power consumption.

Even though they were the most-expensive option for new signals,

many railroads soon began opting for searchlight signals. The single bulb made them energy efficient, and the internal mechanism was protected and more reliable than a semaphore. Searchlights became the most-common signal type installed through the 1970s, replacing many semaphore and old color-light installations.

Although their mechanisms were far less troublesome than semaphore signals, they became problematic enough on older signals that railroads in the past couple of decades have begun opting for color-light signals, and older searchlight signals are rapidly being replaced on many routes.

Position-light signals: The Pennsylvania Railroad developed the position-light signal, introducing the design in 1915. Each round target has seven or nine lights arranged in a circle, with one in the center. Three lights provide each indication, arranged in vertical, horizontal, or either diagonal position, mimicking semaphore aspects. The lamps are a yellowish-white color designed to

This smashboard signal echoes the indication of the dwarf signal at right to protect this crossing on the Chicago & North Western in Madison, Wis. The vertical smashboard extends across the route at far left when the route at right is cleared to cross. *Gordon Odegard*

penetrate fog better than a single colored light.

Another advantage was redundancy, in that one light (two, in some cases) could be out while still providing the signal indication. Some signal heads have individual bulb locations blanked out, or are in a different shape if only one or two aspects are needed.

The signals were used system-wide on the PRR and on affiliated lines (Norfolk & Western and Lehigh Valley). Most remained in service through successor Penn Central and into the Conrail era, but high maintenance costs and their non-standard use of colors meant many

began being replaced starting in the 1980s.

Color position-light signals: Baltimore & Ohio (and affiliates Chicago & Alton and B&O Chicago Terminal) in 1921 added a twist to the position-light design, keeping the circular pattern but eliminating the center bulb and using colors (red, green, yellow) in the appropriate locations. As with the PRR's design, the B&O version has redundancy in that the pattern and color both provide the indication, and one light can be out and still allow the signal to be read. Additional marker lights above and below the main signal head add more

aspects, indicating speeds.

Most color position-light signals survived the Chessie System and CSX mergers, and many are still in service as of 2022.

Dwarf signals: Low-level signals mounted on short masts or on ground platforms are known as dwarf signals. They are typically used in slow-speed trackage, often in interlockings or at control points, such as exiting passing sidings or in yards where they give permission to enter main tracks. Dwarf signals can be almost any signal type; semaphores often use rotating disks instead of conventional arms.

Motor-car signals: Motor-car signals are small, low-mounted signals that indicate track occupancy to work crews aboard motor cars and high-rail trucks. They are small dials mounted on masts or relay cases, often no more than 4 to 6 feet above the ground. Their faces generally rotate, simulating semaphores or position-light signals (as opposed to lights). They are sometimes more widely spaced than lineside signals, and they can show occupancy for multiple blocks.

They're used because speeders and high-rail vehicles don't trigger signal circuits, so they won't trigger approach-lit signals, and trains will not be aware of their presence on a track. They generally provide two indications: occupied and not occupied.

Smashboards: Although more common in Europe, "smashboards" can be found in some installations in the U.S. They are used in conjunction with conventional signals and have a large semaphore-like paddle that has two positions: vertical (clear) or horizontal across the track (stop). They provide both a visual and sound indication—the train striking the signal board. They're most often used at rail crossings and on approaches to moving bridges, often in conjunction with derails.

Signal locations and details

Block signals are located at divisions between signal blocks, usually facing each way on single track on opposite sides of the track. At junctions (interlockings, automatic plants, or

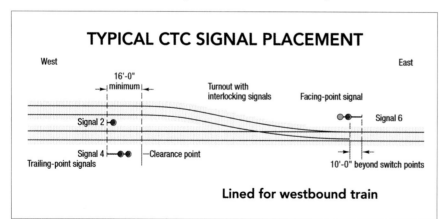

Signal type and placement vary widely depending upon the situation and railroad. This is a typical setup for a siding with dispatcher control using **Centralized Traffic Control.** *Kalmbach Media*

Manually operated signals

Modeled signals can be attention-getters on a model railroad, regardless of the signal type. The animation of colored lights and moving semaphores is fascinating to visitors and operators alike, and great for enhancing layout photography as well.

Even if you're not up to installing a full working signal system on your layout, adding manually controlled signals at one or two locations (such as a junction) provides a great effect. Bulb-only signals can be controlled by toggle or rotary switches. Semaphores can be set using manual turnout linkage, actuated by levers or switches along the fascia or edge of the layout.

You can also add non-operating signals to your layout. Their appearance will add interest and make high-traffic lines more realistic just by their presence. And you always have the option of making them operable in the future as your time and modeling interests allow.

For a complete look at modeling operating signal systems, see Dave Abeles' outstanding book *Guide to Signals & Interlockings* (Kalmbach Media, 2021). For in-depth information on prototype signals, see Brian Solomon's books *Railroad Signaling* (MBI Publishing, 2003) and *Classic Railroad Signals* (Voyageur Press, 2015).

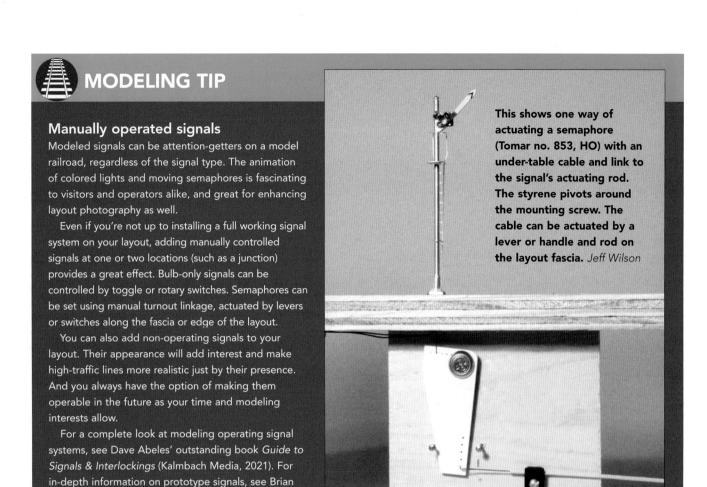

This shows one way of actuating a semaphore (Tomar no. 853, HO) with an under-table cable and link to the signal's actuating rod. The styrene pivots around the mounting screw. The cable can be actuated by a lever or handle and rod on the layout fascia. *Jeff Wilson*

CTC installations), a distant signal generally lets trains know the status of signals at the junction, with a home signal providing absolute permission at the crossing or diverging turnout.

Until 1985, federal rules required signals to be on the right side of the track they controlled—either lineside on the right side of the track or on an overhead signal bridge, above the track they govern. This created some interesting scenes, with secondary tracks sometimes curving sharply to go around signals located between tracks. Many single-track lines now have double-headed signals, with targets facing each direction sharing a common mast.

Passing sidings typically have signals at each end on the main line; at CTC installations, the passing siding often has a dwarf signal where it enters the main line.

Railroads install signal bridges over multi-track locations, as often there

isn't room for individual signal masts between tracks. Their design varies widely among railroads, and includes conventional style (support towers on each side with a truss spanning all tracks) and cantilever style (support post on one side supporting a free arm over the tracks). On cantilever bridges, if signals were not provided for all tracks, a dummy mast or target was added to indicate the unsignaled track or tracks (specific rules for this varied among railroads).

Automatic block and CTC signals long relied on lineside wires (see Chapter 5) to carry electrical messages and codes between blocks and signal locations. Every signal has an equipment case (either at the base of the mast or nearby; see Chapter 6), with a cable running from the communication line to the case.

New signal systems developed in the 1970s use microprocessors to generate and detect codes passed

through the rails themselves, eliminating the need for lineside wires for signaling (Electro Code is one trade name). Some use small satellite dishes or radio signals. By the 2000s, most heavy-traffic lines had shed their lineside wires.

Power for signals has historically been three types: primary (battery only), primary a.c. (from power lines), or a.c. float (batteries, with lineside wires charging the batteries). The type depends on power available at specific locations, with a.c. float preferred wherever electric lines were practical, which expanded greatly in the 1920s and later. Power could come from railroads' own lines, local utilities, buried cables, or solar power.

Railroads sometimes based their signal type by power available. For example, in the 1920s and '30s the Santa Fe used color-light signals (constantly lit) in where primary a.c. was available, but semaphores (which

Train-order signals for opposite directions are usually placed on the same mast. These lower-quadrant semaphores are on Gulf, Mobile & Ohio at the Independence, Mo., station in August 1958. *Paul Larson*

Crossings are sometimes protected by gates of various designs. This gate has multiple lanterns (converted to electric power), a power lock, and a pair of motor-car signals in the cabinet at right. It's at Harrisonville, Mo., on the St. Louis-San Francisco in the 1970s. *TRAINS magazine collection*

used less power) in primary (battery-only) territory.

Many older signals enjoyed long service lives, with some semaphore installations removed in the 2000s having served 80 or more years. The usual reason for upgrading and changing signals is better reliability and more energy-efficient operation.

Train-order signals

Train-order signals—also called "train-order boards" are signals located at depots or interlocking towers staffed by operators. The signals indicate when the operator has written orders to give to the train crew. Whenever train operations deviated from the published schedule—changing the location of a meet, for example—the dispatcher provided written instructions to all involved crews in the form of a train order. The dispatchers dictated the orders to the station operators via telegraph or telephone. The agents would type or write the order on forms, then attach them to hoops and hand them up to engine and caboose crews as they passed.

Train-order signals followed many styles and designs. Most were upper- or lower-quadrant semaphores, but some railroads opted for searchlight or color-light signals. Most railroads used signals with two aspects: Green meant no orders to pick up; red meant picking up orders on the fly.

Some railroads used Form 31 train orders for certain types of orders; these required trains to stop and sign for the orders. These railroads required three-aspect train-order signals—yellow meant picking up orders on the fly; red meant stopping to sign for orders.

As mentioned earlier, in manual block territory these signals were used to convey a train's right to enter the next block. On these lines, train-order signals were ordinarily set at "stop," and were only cleared when a train approached and whistled to call for the signal. Only then did the operator set the signal to "clear"—a safety measure to minimize the risk of a block being cleared inadvertently.

CHAPTER FIVE

Communication lines and poles

They're often simply called "telegraph lines," but the lineside poles and wires that once ran next to almost every railroad line were much more than that. They also handled telephone lines, signal control wires, and electrical power. Although they are disappearing quickly, they were a prominent feature of railroad rights-of-way for more than 100 years.

Amtrak's eastbound *Southwest Chief* rolls past a semaphore on the former Santa Fe (now BNSF) line at Wagon Mound, N. Mex., in December 2018. The code wire is still in service on the line poles to serve the signal system. *Ryan Gaynor*

The Chicago & North Western's branch line at Rewey, Wis., only rated a pair of wires on a simple (no-crossarm) pole line. It was still in place in 1970. *Stan Mailer*

Telegraph systems had been established in the U.S. by the late 1840s, and railroads began using telegraph messages to dispatch trains in 1851. Railroads soon installed poles carrying telegraph wires along most rights-of-way, as railroad stations became the offices for commercial telegraph services (mainly Western Union) as well as their own lines.

By the 1880s, automatic signal systems controlled by rail-based detection circuits were appearing on more and more major routes. These required additional lineside wires for carrying codes among signal installations, and by the 1900s the lines also carried electricity to power them. At the same time, telephone service expanded, and railroad pole lines soon carried their own as well as commercial phone lines.

Trackside pole lines were a good indicator of the traffic level of a railroad. A one-train-a-day branch might have simple two-wire poles carrying a telegraph circuit along the line, or perhaps a single crossarm with

four to six wires. A busy main line, on the other hand, may have lines with three or four 10-pin arms to carry telegraph, telephone, power, and signal lines.

Communication lines remained a staple of most rail routes through the 1960s, but advances in radio communication and the introduction of signal systems that use the rails themselves with microwave or radio to transmit codes led to diminishing numbers of wires on existing lines. By the 1990s, lines were being completely removed from a majority of routes.

We'll look at how lines and poles were built and installed, where they ran, and what functions they supported. We'll also trace their demise, and add a few tips on capturing them realistically on a model railroad.

Pole and line construction

By the early 1900s, poles had evolved to the basic appearance they would retain through the steam and early diesel eras, with one or more multi-pin

crossarms mounted on tall posts.

Poles and crossarms are made from wood, and are treated (generally with creosote), giving new poles a dark brown to black appearance, especially at the base. The top of the pole is cut with either a single or double bevel to aid rain/snow runoff.

Pole height varies depending upon terrain and locale (rural or town/city). From the ground to the bottom arm, a minimum clearance of 18 feet is required over roadways and 25 feet over railroads. Clearance was much lower in other areas, often down to 12 to 14 feet. Poles are tapered, meaning they're thicker at the base (14"-18" diameter) than at the top (10"-14").

The crossarms are seated into notches ("gains") cut into the poles, aiding in alignment and stability. The top crossarm is located 8" to 12" from the top of the pole, with 24" spacing between multiple arms. Arms are bolted in place, with a pair of metal-strap braces in a V shape keeping them aligned.

Although some poles on branch

Although this main line once rated five arms on its communication poles, many wires have been removed by this 1973 view. *Gordon Odegard*

COMMUNICATION LINE TYPICAL PROFILES

Track grade

Berm

18' highway clearance
25' railroad clearance

LEVEL — FILL — CUT — CROSSING — TUNNEL

Lines typically follow the terrain (above). The illustration at right shows a possible arrangement at a station.

Signal
Underground cable
Not to scale
Signal
Relay case
Platform
Station
Cable drop
Crossarm
Drop lines
Wire
Double crossarms
Relay case
Cable drop

---

lines had shorter crossarms, the vast majority of poles along U.S. lines had one or more 10-pin crossarms as the drawings on page 64 show. Not every pin position held an insulator, and not all positions were used. Some branch lines had single-arm poles with 4, 6, or 8 pins; some railroads used arms with 12 or more pins, but they were comparatively rare.

Arm and pin locations were divided and specifically assigned by the service they provided. Each pin location on a pole is numbered, starting with 1 to 10 on the top pole and moving downward. The bottom arm was generally devoted to communication, which could include multiple wires for telegraph circuits and telephone lines.

Up from that is an arm (or more)

dedicated to signal system code lines. Centralized Traffic Control installations required the most wires (and in some cases signal lines had their own pole line, usually on the opposite side of the track). Yet another arm can carry commercial circuits being leased to companies, such as Western Union telegraph or public telephone utilities.

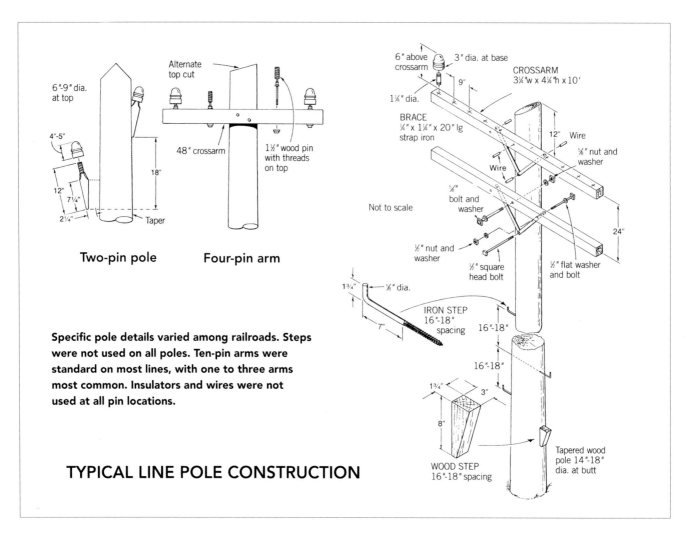

6"-9" dia. at top

4"-5"

12"

7¼"

2¼"

18"

Taper

Two-pin pole

Alternate top cut

48" crossarm

1½" wood pin with threads on top

Four-pin arm

Specific pole details varied among railroads. Steps were not used on all poles. Ten-pin arms were standard on most lines, with one to three arms most common. Insulators and wires were not used at all pin locations.

6" above crossarm

3" dia. at base

9"

CROSSARM 3¼"w x 4¼"h x 10'

1¼" dia.

BRACE ¼" x 1¼" x 20" lg strap iron

12" Wire

⅝" nut and washer

Wire

Not to scale

⅝" bolt and washer

24"

½" nut and washer

½" square head bolt

½" flat washer and bolt

1¾" ⅝" dia.

7"

IRON STEP 16"-18" spacing

16"-18"

16"-18"

1¾" 3"

8"

WOOD STEP 16"-18" spacing

Tapered wood pole 14"-18" dia. at butt

TYPICAL LINE POLE CONSTRUCTION

Low-voltage electric wires—used to power signals and other lineside equipment—rest on their own pins. High-voltage wires (750 to 2,300 volts) are carried on a separate two-pin arm at least 4 feet above the next-lowest communication arm, or may be carried on a separate pole line.

Glass insulators were standard on low-voltage communication and signal lines, and were made in a variety of designs by several manufacturers. Clear, green, and aqua (blue-green) were the most common colors, although there were variations. Threaded wooden dowels ("pins") were mounted on the crossarm; the insulators have hollow, threaded interiors (the pin hole), allowing them to be screwed into place on the pins.

Porcelain insulators were more expensive and thus less common. They were sometimes used for electric supply wires (especially signal or power circuits of 440 volts or higher.

Porcelain was also used where insulators were subject to greater strain, such as tight curves or long spans. These are usually black or brown in color.

Insulators have a slot on their sides—the wire groove—that holds the wire in place. Small lengths of wire, called tie wires, were then wrapped around the line wire and insulator to hold the line wire in place.

Wires were lighter weight than electric utility lines, giving them a noticeably different appearance. Depending upon their service, wires range from 6 AWG (American Wire Gauge) to 14 AWG.

Communication wires were subject to interference ("crosstalk") from neighboring lines if they maintained the same relative positions over long distances. Railroads combated this by transposing pairs of wires every few poles, and transposing other pairs at varying distances. This was done

with a four-insulator transposition bracket or by brackets that held an insulator below the crossarm, allowing neighboring wires to swap positions.

Crossarms would often be doubled on poles that were subject to increased strain, including sharp curves, at the ends of longer-then-standard spans, locations where wires were stub-ended, and locations with connections to other lines or drop lines to relay cabinets and signals.

Some railroads reinforced poles at regular distances. The Great Northern, for example, on its main lines built every tenth pole as an "H fixture," with two vertical poles, paired crossarms, and multiple guy wires. The goal was minimizing overall damage caused by high winds and storms, where one failed pole or downed segment could trigger a domino-effect toppling of miles of line.

Crossarms alternate sides on every pole to minimize strain: if you're looking at a pole line from the side, and one pole has the arms on the left side, the next pole will have them on the right, and so on. Poles climbing hills will all have their crossarms on the uphill side of each pole, often with a double-arm pole at the summit.

Spacing between poles varied by railroad, with 40 poles per mile common (132-foot spacing; every four poles is a tenth of a mile), but some railroads used other spacing, including 50 poles per mile (106-foot spacing). On model railroads, making this spacing tighter seems to look better, and many modelers feel this enhances the feeling of distance along track.

Poles are typically placed about 20 feet from the nearest rail. In towns this distance can become tighter; obstructions (man-made or natural) can require railroads to route lines around various features. The drawing on page 63 shows a typical station arrangement, with poles going around

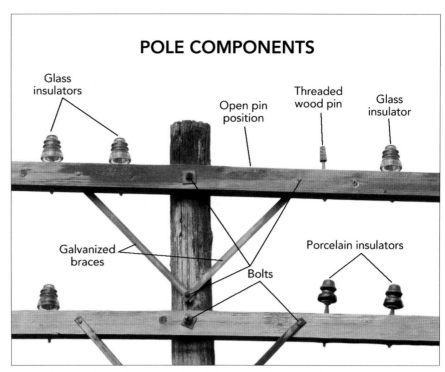

POLE COMPONENTS

This out-of-service pole has weathered to gray with several shades of brown highlights. It has both glass and porcelain insulators; all pin positions were not used. *Jeff Wilson*

The pole line along the Union Pacific in Nebraska still carries some code wires in 2006. The top arm carries high-voltage electric wires (single-phase a.c.) to power signals and equipment. *Jeff Wilson*

Along its main lines, the Great Northern used double-post (H-fixture), double-crossarm, multi-guy-wire poles at every 10th pole. Reinforced poles were often used on curves, long spans, and locations where cables or wires branched off. *Jeff Wilson*

the station; other locations have the lines going directly over the structure.

Communication lines typically follow the undulations of the surrounding terrain, so pole lines follow hills where the railroad grade passes through cuts, atop fills, or through short tunnels. Long tunnels may have lines cabled to pass through. Long bridges and trestles typically have arms mounted on bridge members to carry the lines.

Guy wires are used on poles on curves as needed, where the tension of the wires would pull the pole inward. If a guy wire can't be used because of obstructions, an alternate is to use a back brace, a pole driven into the ground at an angle to keep the line pole vertical.

Signal and communication lines must be connected (dropped) to many trackside structures and devices, including lineside signals, crossing signals, stations, interlocking towers, powered turnouts (and derails), phone booths, relay cases, and instrument cabinets. At these locations, wires are

This reinforced double-arm pole has a cable running to the equipment shed in the background. Also at this passing siding location are a propane tank, switch heater (behind the tank), base for an antenna (at left), and two-head searchlight signal (at right). *Jeff Wilson*

Back braces are used on poles under stress from wires pulling to the side, as this pole on a curve. *Donald Sims*

Transposition brackets were sets of four insulators that allowed wires to swap positions. One is still in service on this pole; two others are out of service, with their wires cut. *Jeff Wilson*

A bundled cable drop goes from a reinforced (double crossarm, guy wires) pole to a semaphore along the Santa Fe main line in Missouri in 1943. *Jack Delano, Library of Congress*

MODELING TIP

Stringing wire: pros and cons

Adding poles along a model right-of-way certainly goes a long way toward realism. Modelers have long debated whether to add simulated wires to their modeled poles. When done well, scale lines can look great and add to the authenticity of a scene. Adding wires is a time-consuming task, however, and done poorly—with wires that appear too heavy or that kink or sag unrealistically—they can detract from realism.

Modelers have tried many materials for lines, including cotton or nylon thread, monofilament, fine wire, and elastic line (Lycra thread). Common thread can appear heavy, and although fine monofilament has a lighter appearance, both can be difficult to string multiple lines with

Bill Aldrich strung the five-arm pole line on his HO scale New Haven Shore Line layout with .003" Lycra elastic thread. The results are impressive and quite realistic, especially when coupled with working signals and other trackside details. *Paul Dolkos*

equal tension to avoid sagging. Among the best materials is elastic thread such as EZ Line, made by Berkshire Junction, or other Lycra threads. The stretchy nature of the material allows applying it slightly in tension. It can be glued to insulators with super glue.

Some manufacturers—including Rapido and Woodland Scenics—have offered poles pre-strung with wires.

The bottom line for modelers is often the overall scope and size of the potential installation. Modeling lines works well for small scenes or layouts, or longer scenes with fewer wires. A long shelf-style layout of a branch line with four wires on

single crossarms is a more doable project than the same layout featuring a main line with three 10-pin arms full of wires (but it's certainly possible, as the above photo of Bill Aldrich's layout shows).

Whichever option you choose, whenever possible locate the communication line on the side of the tracks opposite of aisles and viewing areas. Looking through poles and lines to see the trains is distracting (just like in real life!) for viewers and for photography, and poles and lines can easily be damaged when reaching into scenes to uncouple trains, line turnouts, or perform maintenance.

---

tapped as needed at a neighboring pole and routed to the device. This was usually done by a bundled, insulated cable strung to an extended pole atop the relay case or structure. You can see several examples of this in this chapter as well as Chapter 4.

Evolution and demise

Pole lines were expensive to maintain, both in terms of the equipment (tens of thousands of poles, thousands of miles of wire, millions of insulators, plus assorted other hardware) and for the labor they needed to keep them operable. Lines were subject to damage from storms (especially ice and wind), vandalism, theft, and accidents.

Lightning could wreak havoc with signal and communication systems.

Railroads continued using telegraph for dispatching and other communications through the 1940s, but by the 1950s the telephone and teletype had taken over for many of these operations. Even though many railroads retained their telegraph circuits for quite some time, most discontinued telegraph operations by the end of the 1960s.

Railroads began using microwave communications in the late 1950s, eliminating many wires. New technology and circuit design allowed placing more communications and codes in fewer wires, also eliminating wires.

The switch from timetable-and-train order operations to track warrants and other systems made possible by direct radio communications between dispatchers and train crews eliminated the need for station operators, and many were gone by the 1970s. Railroads began using commercial telephone services for remaining operations instead of railroads' own systems.

By this time, much of the traffic that remained was now carried on bundled cable lines, similar to that used by telephone and cable operators.

The 1980s saw the growth of new signal systems that relied on coded information sent through the

The pole line elevates to change sides on the Santa Fe in Kansas in 1943, with reinforced, double-crossarm poles. A drop cable starts at the pole at right, continues to the next pole and a short pole, then to an equipment box at the signal bridge. There's also a motor-car setoff in the foreground at right. *Jack Delano, Library of Congress*

rails themselves, along with radio communication (more on that in Chapter 4), meaning lineside wires were no longer needed for signaling. The only need remaining was providing electrical power to signals, but this is now done in most locations by local utilities instead of railroad lines. As railroads have continued upgrading their signal systems, especially on primary routes, the need for pole lines vanished by the 2000s.

As services dwindled from the 1960s to the 1980s, individual wires were typically removed as they were taken out of service by cutting them at insulators (wire being valuable as scrap), and crossarms were sometimes removed as well if all of their wires were removed. This left many lines with a stripped-down appearance, having multiple crossarms with few wires remaining. Bundled cables were often carried below the lowest crossarm.

When all wires were out of service, pole lines are generally completely removed—especially on high-traffic routes. Wires are taken down and poles are cut down and hauled off by contractors. Poles along secondary and branch lines are sometimes abandoned in place, with removal only if they interfere with traffic or new construction.

Effectively modeling pole lines means understanding how they were used along the railroad you're modeling, in particular for the specific era you're modeling. Following prototype photos can help with this. Commercial poles can be painted, detailed, and modified; some modelers even choose to model the lines themselves, as the sidebar on page 68 explains.

CHAPTER SIX

Cases, cabinets, detectors, and details

A BNSF double-stack train passes a communication installation at Siberia, Calif., in 2015. The equipment includes a microwave tower, PTC (Positive Train Control) antennas, equipment sheds, propane tank, signals, chain-link fencing, and electric (non-railroad-owned) lines. *Scott A. Hartley*

Keeping trains running requires a tremendous variety of lineside equipment sheds and cases, scanners and detectors of various types; and track components such as derails, rail lubricators, and guardrails. Adding these details to a layout will help convey the idea that you're modeling a real, working railroad.

Equipment cases and phone booths

They're often called "relay cases," but equipment sheds, cabinets, and cases hold all manner of electrical control equipment, keeping it safe from the elements but accessible for maintenance. Every location with powered signals—block signals, Centralized Traffic Control signals, grade crossing gates and flashers, and powered turnouts—requires one or more nearby equipment sheds to hold equipment.

Early versions were cast iron boxes with panel doors, and could be rectangular or have rounded tops. Many were small, just 14" to 20" wide, a foot deep, and 24" tall, often mounted on cast-iron pipe for a post or sometimes integrated to the base of a signal mast. Railroads often built sheds to their own designs, with concrete or wood construction in various sizes.

By the 1930s, cases were becoming larger as signal installations grew more numerous and more complex. Prefabricated versions were offered by manufacturers by the 1940s, which typically featured sheet-metal construction and range in size from cabinets to walk-in sheds. Cabinets are generally about 24" deep and 4 to 10 feet wide. Walk-in sheds are 6 feet wide, 8, 10, or 12 feet long, and 8 feet tall.

Lineside signals sometimes have equipment cases as part of the base; early semaphores had their motor mechanisms in the base, and even after the mechanisms were moved, had cabinets with one or two compartments for relays and batteries.

Keeping equipment dry is vital, so cabinets and sheds rest on concrete bases. Small cases are often elevated 12" or more above ground level by either a solid concrete slab or by a pair of concrete pedestals. Larger sheds are on concrete pads or metal posts, elevated to avoid standing water.

Through the 1980s, cases and sheds were located next to a lineside pole, with a cable drop from the pole to the shed—often using a short pole or mast attached to or next to the shed.

Every signal requires an equipment cabinet or shed. This one is mounted on concrete pedestals, with a cable to the line pole. A cylindrical battery vault is at left. All modern grade crossings are labeled with their location and unique number; a contact phone number is on the other (street) side of the cabinet. *Jeff Wilson*

Walk-in equipment sheds are generally 6 feet wide and 8 to 12 feet long. This one has two cables to a neighboring line pole and a communications antenna (projecting from the roof at rear). It rests on metal footings. *Jeff Wilson*

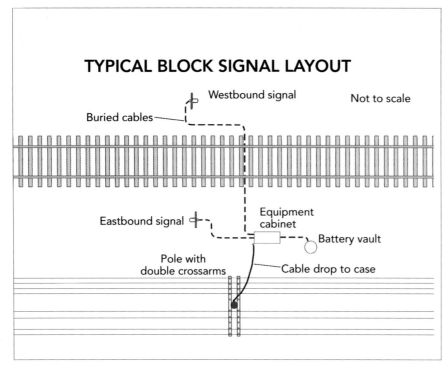

TYPICAL BLOCK SIGNAL LAYOUT

Westbound signal

Not to scale

Buried cables

Eastbound signal

Equipment cabinet

Battery vault

Pole with double crossarms

Cable drop to case

Equipment layout varies by location, but a typical layout for block signals has a cable drop to an equipment case, with buried cables to a neighboring battery vault and to the signals. *Jeff Wilson*

Early phone booths were often full enclosures, as with this concrete version on a Conrail (former Erie) line in Ohio in 1986. *John Ciccarelli*

Connections from the case to the signal and battery vault is by underground cable. By the 1990s, lineside pole lines were disappearing (see Chapter 5). Signal codes are now transmitted by rail; additional communications can be by radio, microwave, or satellite dish; power can come from a local utility line (which can be underground as well).

Near each equipment shed will be a battery well (or "vault" or "cellar"). Signals are powered by batteries, but since the 1930s most also have a.c. line power to charge batteries and provide a constant backup (called "a.c. float"). The battery well is a reinforced, waterproof concrete box, usually cylindrical (although some are square) with a locked cover. Cables run out of the vault above ground level but then enter the ground. Vault size varies by installation, protruding about 18" above ground and typically 30" in diameter or greater.

Since the 1990s, cabinets and sheds at grade crossings are labeled with the crossing name, identification number (unique to that crossing), and an 800 number that can be called in case of an accident or vehicle blocking the crossing.

Another common lineside installation is the phone booth or box. Lineside telephones were especially important into the 1960s and earlier, before direct radio communications between dispatcher and train crews became common. Phones were located at the ends of sidings, at junctions, crossings, and other interlockings, at defect detectors, and many signals— locations where a train might be stopped or delayed. The phones were generally the railroads' own systems, and they enabled a train crew to call the dispatcher directly, or to call a nearby interlocking tower or station.

Some phone enclosures were full booths, typically about 3 feet square and 7 feet tall. More common were small enclosures or cabinets ("phone boxes") mounted on their own posts or on the posts of a neighboring pole line. Phone boxes could be wood, but by the late steam era were usually metal. They had locked covers to limit access and keep out rain and snow.

A Union Pacific crew member uses a lineside phone box to call the dispatcher from where his train is stopped at a block signal in 1977. The wood box is mounted to a line pole. *Steve Patterson*

This metal Milwaukee Road phone box is mounted on a wood pole along tracks in Milwaukee in 1973. Phone boxes are secured with padlocks. *Gordon Odegard*

ACI and AEI scanners

Through the 1960s, keeping track of where freight cars were required teams of clerks tracking waybills and car lists. Train consists were transmitted among terminals via telegraph and later via teletype, but tracking down cars sometimes required clerks to hike down long lines of freight cars in yards or sidings.

In the 1960s, railroads through the Association of American Railroads (AAR) made their first attempt at an automated system that could scan passing cars. The Automatic Car Identification (ACI) system, developed by GTE (and marketed as KarTrak) required bar-code-style plates (10" x 22") with reflective color-stripes to be mounted to all rolling stock and locomotives. The system debuted in 1967. Applying the labels took a long time, and by 1975, about 90 percent of cars were equipped.

Trackside optical readers were installed at hundreds of locations across the country, usually on main tracks approaching yards and junctions (see a typical installation at right, and the illustration on page 74) where trains originated and terminated. The optical scanners were located in boxes mounted on posts, with a hood over the opening for the scanner.

The ACI system proved unsuccessful. The biggest problem was grime: Freight cars get dirty, and the optical readers couldn't read the barcodes covered with grime. By 1977, when the system was abandoned, 95

This ACI (KarTrak) scanner is near Milwaukee in 1977. The optical system read colored bar code panels on the side of each freight car. The problem of road grime couldn't be solved, and the system was abandoned in 1977. *Gordon Odegard*

ACI (KARTRAK) SCANNER

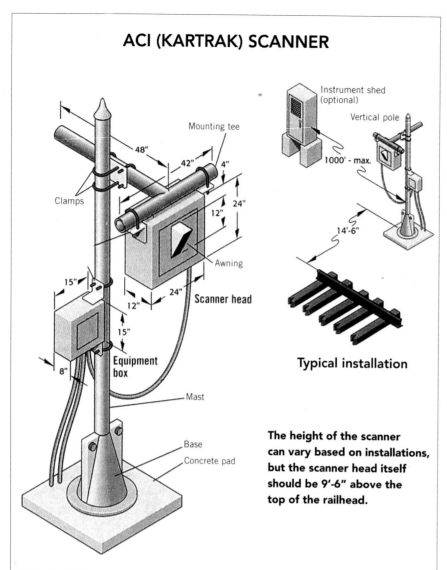

Mounting tee

48"

42"

4"

Clamps

24"

12"

15"

24"

Awning

12"

Scanner head

15"

Equipment box

8"

Mast

Base

Concrete pad

Instrument shed (optional)

Vertical pole

1000' - max.

14'-6"

Typical installation

The height of the scanner can vary based on installations, but the scanner head itself should be 9'-6" above the top of the railhead.

AEI SCANNER

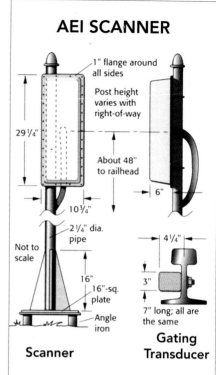

1" flange around all sides

Post height varies with right-of-way

29¼"

About 48" to railhead

6"

10¾"

2¼" dia. pipe

Not to scale

16"

16"-sq. plate

Angle iron

Scanner

4¼"

3"

7" long; all are the same

Gating Transducer

The AEI (Automatic Equipment Identification) system has been in use since the mid-1990s. Scanners use radio waves to get information from the passive-radio receivers mounted on each freight car. *Kalmbach Media*

percent of cars were equipped but the fail rate was 20 percent—not efficient enough to make the system worthwhile. Although most scanners were soon removed from service, labels remained on cars and could still be found well into the 2000s, when cars of that era were being retired.

The next attempt at an automatic scanning system was much more successful. Adopted in 1991, the AEI (automatic equipment identification) system uses passive radio signals instead of optics, meaning dirt and grime were no longer an impediment to operation.

Data tags are affixed to the frame on each side of all freight cars. Each tag is an unpowered (passive) radio transponder that, in its circuitry, includes reporting marks, car number, and equipment type. The devices are enclosed in hard-plastic housings roughly 3 x 10 inches, with tapered ends, and are usually left unpainted gray.

The trackside AEI scanners project

DRAGGING EQUIPMENT DETECTOR

Flaps bolted to rotating bar. Tops of 4 inside flaps (about 9" high) are even with bottom of railhead. Outside flaps are 1" higher.

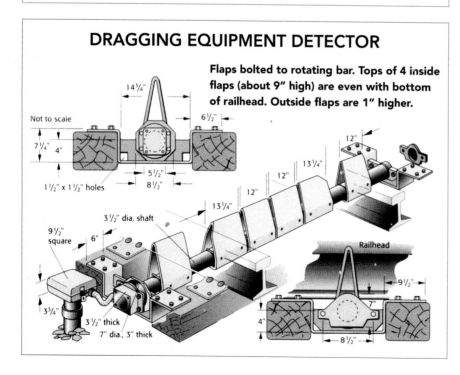

14¾"

6½"

Not to scale

7¼"   4"

5½"

8½"

1½" x 1½" holes

12"

13¼"

12"

12"

13¼"

Railhead

3½" dia. shaft

9½" square

6"

9½"

3¾"

3½" thick

7" dia., 3" thick

7"

4"

8½"

Motor-car setout

Motor-car setouts are easy to model. This HO example is simply two pieces of scale 10 x 10 stripwood, stained, glued in place at right angles to the track, with additional vertical stripwood posts for support. Thin stripwood is glued between the rails. The speeder model is a white-metal kit from Durango Press. Typical setout locations include interlocking towers, ends of sidings, junctions, and at block signals.

A motor car ("speeder") rests on a setout next to the interlocking tower at Portage, Ill., on my old HO scale Chicago, Burlington & Quincy. *Jeff Wilson*

a radio signal to reflect and modulate the information back to the reader. Readers are boxy structures mounted on stands; they're often located near other detector equipment.

Railroads began applying tags to cars in early 1992, with a goal of having all cars tagged by the end of 1994. More than 3,000 trackside scanners were in service by 2000. The system has been extremely successful, with an accuracy rate of nearly 100 percent.

Defect detectors

Through most of the steam era, detecting mechanical problems with moving trains—such as overheated bearings, broken wheels, and dragging or broken equipment—was dependent upon on-board crews' observations. Station operators and other employees were also required to provide rolling inspections to passing trains and give a highball signal to the caboose crew as the train passed if all was well. Unfortunately, crews and trackside observers were often unable to detect problems until damage had already occurred.

The solution was a series of in-track and trackside detectors that could automatically check passing trains for various defects. Since the 1940s, this has included a combination of dragging-equipment detectors and hot-bearing

This BNSF installation in 2014 includes a dragging-equipment detector (paddles in foreground) as well as a hot-bearing detector (outside the rail at left) and a pair of wheel counters (inside the rail opposite the bearing detector. *Tom Kline*

("hotbox") detectors, and modern devices can analyze a variety of data on moving trains. Automated detectors became especially important after the elimination of cabooses from the 1980s onward, as crew members no longer keep an eye on the train from the rear.

Dragging-equipment detectors began appearing in the 1940s, and improved designs led to their increased

use in the 1960s and later. They're designed to identify any obstruction hanging from the train—such as broken brake gear, a loose brake shoe, a broken wheel, or a derailed car—as all present a serious hazard. Initial designs used a thin, breakable bar between the rails just below railtop level—called a "brittle bar"—that carried a low-level electrical current. A low-hanging

A worker checks a hotbox detector on Union Pacific near Omaha. The ramps on either side of the detector protect it from dragging equipment. *Union Pacific*

obstruction would break the bar, breaking the circuit and alerting the dispatcher.

By the 1960s, detectors were redesigned with a series of moveable, sprung paddles outside and between the rails. The paddles extend from a rod under the base of the rail upward to just below rail-top level. Dangling equipment will push a paddle over, as will the wheel of a derailed car, triggering the detector. This design required less maintenance and was more effective than earlier designs.

To alert crews, early installations relied on lineside signals placed at least a train length from the detector, with a restrictive signal requiring the crew to stop and check for defects. Some detectors communicated directly with the dispatcher, who activated a signal; later installations did this directly. A variation by the 1970s was a detector that provided a digital readout of

This Canadian Pacific detector, in Ontario in 1983, displays a digital readout of an axle number for a defect. *Canadian Pacific*

the axle or car number that triggered the detector. Modern detectors use an automated radio announcement intended for the engine crew, giving the detector location and either an all clear message or an axle count of the defect.

Overheated axle bearings were a major problem for railroads in the days of solid-bearing journals. If a journal box ran dry and overheated, the result was often a fire, and it could result in axle failure and a derailment. The coming of roller bearings in the 1960s greatly reduced the problem, but they can fail as well.

Hotbox (hot bearing) detectors began appearing in the mid-1950s, using infrared sensors in a scanner head mounted outside each rail. They were designed to provide an alarm if a bearing was above a certain temperature (usually 180 degrees above ambient temperature). They proved their worth immediately: an early installation on the Boston & Maine in 1957 detected 52 hotboxes in its first five months of operation, most of which had not been noticed by train crews.

As with dragging-equipment detectors, early hotbox detectors reported to local operators or

Early defect detectors used signals to alert train crews of problems. This signal at Camden, Ohio, on Norfolk & Western in 1979 had two indications: green for proceed; red for "call dispatcher." *Philip A. Deacon*

dispatchers, then to lineside signals, and eventually via radio communication to crews.

Dragging-equipment and hotbox detectors are often grouped together at the same location (see page 78). Specific placement and frequency varies by railroad and region. High-

traffic main lines often have detectors every 12 to 20 miles.

Since 2000, several additional types of detectors have begun appearing along railroads. Acoustic bearing detectors and multiple high-speed, high-definition cameras capture the sounds and appearance of passing

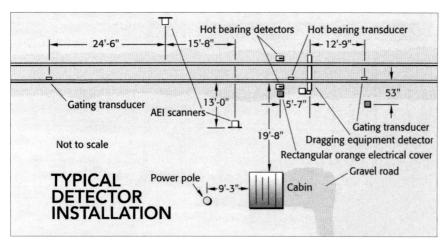

TYPICAL DETECTOR INSTALLATION

Not to scale

Hot bearing detectors — Hot bearing transducer

Gating transducer — AEI scanners — Dragging equipment detector — Rectangular orange electrical cover — Gating transducer — Gravel road — Cabin — Power pole

24'-6" 15'-8" 12'-9" 13'-0" 5'-7" 19'-8" 53" 9'-3"

Detectors of various types are often grouped together at a single location. Here's a possible layout. *Kalmbach Media*

cars; a microprocessor compares the detector's results to standards. This allows detection of many defects before they become hazards, including worn bearings, loose hopper gates, flat and defective wheels, and misaligned trucks.

There are also detectors that can analyze truck performance and identify problems or potential problems. Infrared detectors can now also identify overheated wheels, which can indicate sticking brakes.

High-and-wide load detectors use stereo imaging to accurately plot the overall dimensions of passing cars,

Cattle guards

Grazing pastures, especially on large ranches and open ranges in the west, sometimes overlapped railroad tracks. Where fences crossed the tracks, cattle guards were installed to keep animals from crossing boundaries. These included an angled fence to the base of the ends of the ties, along with some type of low obstructions to keep livestock from getting footing at the crossing (conventional ties protruding from the ballast or metal bars).

TRAINS magazine collection

This wheel impact load detector, on BNSF double-track near Cochrane, Wis., in 2006, can spot potential problems with wheels, trucks, and bearings. *Steve Glischinski*

This wedge-style derail is controlled by a ground throw on a headblock, similar to a turnout. It's aligned to derail cars coming from the side opposite the derail. *Gordon Odegard*

This wedge derail is controlled by a high-level switch stand, and also has a separate "derail" sign. It's on a spur connecting to the BNSF main line in Minnesota. *Jeff Wilson*

and can flag cars that are too large to clear upcoming obstructions (such as tunnels or bridges), or loads that have shifted and are now sticking out from the train.

Derails

Derails are used to prevent car and train movements into areas where they could cause collisions and damage greater than a simple derailment. They've been used on industrial spurs, at junctions and interlockings, and at approaches to moving bridges.

Derails are made in many designs and sizes, but they are of two types: wedge and split rail. A wedge derail is a heavy cast block that rests on top of one of the running rails, with a wedge-shaped angle that guides the wheel flange of a car up and over the rail. Some ("universal") derails have a V-shaped wedge and will work either direction; others are directional, and must be installed so the wedge faces the proper direction.

Some wedge derails are hinged—they flip to the inside (between the rails) and down to clear the rail. Most wedge derails are retractable ("sliding"), where the wedge or shoe slides inward off the rail. There are also portable

Split-rail derails look like half of a turnout. This one, on the St. Louis-San Francisco at Neosho, Mo., is controlled by the operator at an interlocking plant and protects a crossing. The extended guardrail is designed to keep equipment upright. *Harold K. Vollrath collection*

derails, placed by maintenance crews on the boundaries of the track zones on which they're working.

Wedge derails are sized to fit specific rail sizes. Regulations specify that they must be visible, and since the 1960s it's been common to paint them, usually yellow or orange. They're controlled like a turnout, either with a manual switch stand or electric switch motor.

Split-rail derails look like half of a turnout. A point, lined by a switch stand or electric switch motor, is

opened, guiding cars or trains off the right of way. These were the type most often used on mainline tracks at interlockings and junctions, although their use has declined since the 1940s. Derails on mainline tracks often included a long guardrail extension, to aid in keeping derailed equipment upright.

The most common derail locations are on industrial spurs, between the car spots and the turnout that connects to the main line or switching lead track. A current BNSF guideline

This derail has two points and is controlled by an electric switch machine. It directs cars away from the main line, but does not include a frog. *TRAINS magazine collection*

Bridge decks are the most common location for guardrails, as here on the Monon near Cedar Lake, Ind., in the 1940s. *TRAINS magazine collection*

for industrial trackage specifies that a derail must be used on all tracks that connect with a main line, siding, or industrial lead. The derail should be located so that it guides the car away from the mainline track. If the mainline turnout is powered, the derail must also be powered.

Derails should be placed on tangent (straight) track whenever possible; if it's on curved track, the derail should be installed on the outside rail. A common requirement is that the derail be at least 100 feet from the fouling point of a mainline turnout or 50 feet from the fouling point of a turnout on a switch lead or secondary track (we can cut this distance a bit on a layout without losing realism).

The other common derail location is at junctions where rail lines cross each other or on an approach track to a moveable (swing, bascule, or lift) bridge. These derails are tied to interlocking signals (or Centralized Traffic Control systems), so that the derail can't be opened until the signals are cleared for a particular route. These are most commonly split rail derails on main tracks and wedge derails on low-speed tracks.

A sign is required at all derail locations. Signs vary in style by railroad and era.

Guardrails

Guardrails run inside and parallel to the running rails to keep any derailed equipment from leaving the tracks where it could cause excessive damage. The most common locations are across bridges and trestles, but you'll also find them in tunnels, at grade crossings, passing under bridges, and near stations and platforms.

Guardrails are usually lighter rail than the running rail, and guardrails are spiked in place without tie plates, giving them a lower profile. Guardrails are curved inward at each end; in some locations, they form a point like a turnout frog.

Modeling guardrails is easy. As with the prototype, use smaller rail, bending the ends to match prototype usage. Guardrails can be either glued or spiked in place.

Two telltales of differing designs stand over Elgin, Joliet & Eastern tracks at Rondout, Ill., in the 1940s, protecting crews from a bridge behind the photographer. *Linn H. Westcott*

This flange lubricator is on Conrail near East Brookfield, Mass., in 1993. The between-rails pipes show the location, with the railtop-level channels for the applicators. The surrounding tracks are coated liberally in grease. *Jeff Wilson*

Telltales

Through the steam and early diesel eras, telltales were found all across the railroad landscape. They consisted of an over-track bracket with multiple ropes hanging down. They were designed to warn crewmen riding atop cars of approaching above-track obstructions, and were placed in advance of almost all bridges, tunnels, sheds, and station canopies. A crewman feeling the ropes brushing against him knew to duck immediately to avoid the obstruction.

In the days before portable radios were common, crew members often rode on top of cars to relay hand

Assorted scrap and junk is often found next to the tracks, including rail hardware, brake shoes, air hoses, and other details. *Gordon Odegard*

Westbound Wabash freight ADK-1, behind a new GE U25B, rolls past a motor-car setout next to JA Tower at Jacksonville, Ill., in May 1962. *J. David Ingles*

signals to each other, or they would walk the train while it was in motion, checking for mechanical problems. Brakemen would also ride on top of cars that had been shoved during switching moves, applying the handbrakes to stop them.

Telltale construction varied widely among railroads (and even individual installations). Most common was a vertical wood post or metal (pipe or rail) pole with a braced arm extending over the track. Some looked like they were cobbled together on site from random materials; others were quite ornate. Multi-track installations often had poles on either side with a cable across the track.

As can be imagined, riding atop cars was dangerous in the best conditions. By the late 1950s, increased use of radio communications and lineside defect detectors eliminated much of the need for crew members to ride cars; in 1964 running boards were no longer required on new cars and shortly thereafter railroads were required to remove them from older cars. Telltales were removed or, in some cases, abandoned in place; many could still be seen into the late 1900s.

Flange and rail lubricators

An often overlooked detail are the prototype devices that add grease to wheel treads and flanges. Friction between wheels and rails—especially on curves—causes excessive wear to both, and requires more power to haul trains. Where and when to add grease has been the subject of much scientific study among railroads: too much lubrication can cause locomotive wheels to slip and decrease traction; too little results in excessive wear. Railroads use them because they work extremely well: lubricators have doubled and tripled rail life at some locations.

The most common locations for lubricators is just before the beginning of sharp curves (or multiple curves), especially on grades, where wear issues are compounded. You'll find them every few miles in curved, mountainous areas on lines that see frequent, heavy traffic.

Automatic flange greasers have been in use since the 1930s. The first devices were actuated by a button on the outside of a rail. As locomotive and car wheel treads rolled across the button, the device pumped lubricant inside the rail at the flangeway. Specific designs vary, with some applying lubricant on both rails and some to one rail only (the outside rail, as it is subject to greater wear). Early lubricators were directly activated, with the wheel depressing a plunger that powered the pump.

The lubricant is in sealed tank or container, usually buried below ground level at or next to the lubricator. Newer installations are electrically powered (line power or solar) and are able to better regulate the amount of grease applied. They don't depend upon direct wheel contact to actuate the pump. Since the 1990s, railroads have begun

Railroad rights-of-way often host buried cable and fiber optic lines, marked with signs and posts. This one, in 2017, stands in front of the technology it replaced: an old communications pole that now holds only a mile marker, but no wires. *Tom Kline*

using top-of-rail lubrication in many areas as well.

With either type of lubricator, the telltale signs along the tracks are the heavy, dark, oily areas along the track that stretch outward from the device. The ends of the hoses and delivery pipes are often visible, along with what looks like a guardrail inside the running rail. The devices themselves can be difficult to see, because they're usually heavily coated in lubricant, and blend in with the dark color of the track.

Additional details

The list of potential details is quite long.

General junk and debris can be found almost anywhere—cut-off sections of rail, old spikes and tie plates, discarded or broken signal equipment, and old signs to name a few. These shouldn't be left in locations where they would become a hazard for crew members walking along the tracks.

Motor-car setouts were once quite common along most lines. Railroad maintenance crews once depended on speeders (motor cars) to travel along the rails to perform inspection and repairs. These vehicles were lightweight, and could be removed from the track by hand by crew members. Railroads

A weathered barbed-wire fence traces the edge of the right of way along the Union Pacific main line in Nebraska. You'll find fences of various kinds paralleling railroad tracks. *Jeff Wilson*

This snow fence along the Union Pacific in Wyoming is designed to break the wind, limiting the amount of snow that piles up on the neighboring track. *Harry Brunk*

warning not to dig along the line.

Train communication antennas, antennas for microwave communications, and installations for positive train control (PTC) are appearing along train lines across the country.

Fences of various types can be found along right-of-way borders. This includes barbed-wire and electric fences in many rural areas, with chain-link, board, and ornamental metal fences in towns and urban locales. Snow fences are used in many areas in the prairies and foothills.

As with other features, these details will vary widely by railroad, region, and era. Keep your eyes open when traveling along prototype track, and study photos for details lurking in the background. Anything you can add will make your model right-of-way more realistic.

provided locations (setouts) for this every few miles along the line where crews could easily clear the main line.

The setouts are made from pairs of rails or heavy timbers (spaced at the rail gauge), positioned at 90 degrees to the tracks, with enough room to park a car fully in the clear. Timbers between the rails aided in moving the speeders. Setouts became rare by the late 1900s,

as speeders gave way to high-rail trucks (pickups or large trucks equipped with both highway and rail wheels), which enter and leave the tracks at grade crossings.

Many rail lines serve as rights-of-way for buried cable and fiber optic lines, either owned by the railroad or leased to a contractor. These will have signs and markers along the route

CHAPTER SEVEN

Highway and street crossings and details

There are more than 125,000 public grade crossings in the U.S.—plus another 80,000 private crossings—where railroad tracks cross streets, roads, and highways. Along with the mechanical aspects of building crossings that allow highway vehicles to cross railroads are the myriad warning signs and signals that have been used through the years.

A Rock Island doodlebug rolls its branchline freight across a grade crossing near Powhattan, Kan., in May 1962. The oiled gravel road and crossbuck with beaded lettering, "Look out for the cars" lettering and railroad signboard set the tone for the scene as much as the train itself. *Frank Tatnall*

85

The Illinois Central placed large crossbucks and warning signs in the middle of this gravel road—surrounded by a low wall of whitewashed rocks—to warn traffic at this rural crossing. The scene dates to around 1900. *Illinois Central*

A northbound Atlantic Coast Line train passes a non-standard crossing sign north of Weldon, N.C., in 1950. *Atlantic Coast Line*

We'll start with a look at the history and evolution of grade crossings, see how crossings were once guarded by watchmen and manually operated gates, then look at how automatic signals and gates took over. We'll also look at the materials historically used to build grade crossings and see the most common types of crossings today.

Because the methods and materials involved have changed so much since the late 1800s, knowing what's appropriate for a given era is key in capturing grade crossings realistically on a layout.

Crossings are either active or passive. Active crossings have some type of signal (bell, lights) or gates that are activated as trains approach. Passive crossings have signs only.

Non-standard crossing signs include, from left, an angled sign on Central Vermont in 1945; cast oval sign as used on the Pennsylvania and others; cast oval sign on concrete post on the New Haven; diamond-shaped sign on New York Central; and a plain rectangular sign on the Aberdeen & Rockfish in 1978. *Photos, from left: Edwin A. Wilde; Trains magazine collection; Kent Day Coes; New York Central; Mike Small*

There have been countless variations of the crossbuck sign over the years, including (from left) Lehigh & New England with ornate wood boards on concrete post, 1940s; Santa Fe with "Look out ..." and railroad lettering, 1943; standard 50-degree angled on Milwaukee Road, 1970s; with French lettering in Canada, 1954; "Railway" Crossing, Canada (Saskatchewan), 1981; and modern 90-degree with reflectorized post on Union Pacific. *Photos, from left: Kent Day Coes; Jack Delano, Library of Congress; Gordon Odegard; Philip R. Hastings; Len Thompson; Jeff Wilson*

Crossbucks and warning signs

The now-familiar highway railroad crossing sign, with two signboards placed in an "X" with "RAILROAD CROSSING" lettering, is familiar, and is an excellent graphic representation of the crossing itself. Although it has been the virtual standard for grade crossings since the early 1900s, there have been hundreds of variations on it.

Signs were in many shapes, as the accompanying photos show. The Pennsylvania Railroad used oval cast-iron signs with "RAILROAD CROSSING, STOP, LOOK, AND LISTEN," lettering. Some of these lasted into the 1960s.

The New York Central used diamond-shaped boards with "LOOK OUT FOR THE CARS" lettering. Other railroads used plain rectangular sign boards or boards at angles.

Crossbucks came in many variations. Most early versions used a pair of boards at a shallow angle (50 or 60 degrees). Almost all had "RAILROAD CROSSING" lettering, but some added "LOOK OUT FOR THE CARS" or similar wording, either on one of the angled boards or on the post itself. Signboards at a 90-degree angle became more common starting in the late 1930s, and is the standard today.

The style of lettering and shape of the sign boards also varied. Some were ornate, with angled ends and outlining. Sign posts also varied. Many railroads opted for concrete posts, often with diagonal black-and-white striping. The sign boards would sometimes be located on the same side of the post; other railroads applied one board to each side of the post, giving them a distinctive appearance. Other signs were mounted on wood or metal (pipe) posts.

Lettering was typically black on white. Reflective glass beads became common on lettering in the 1930s to increase nighttime visibility, and some

A stop sign with a separate rectangular crossing sign has become standard for private railroad crossings since the 1990s. *Thomas E. Hoffmann*

A pedestrian waits as the crossing watchman (right) holds his stop sign to flag traffic as a Union Pacific streamliner sails through Geneva, Ill., in the early 1940s. The crossing shanty has a manual bell over the door, with a "Third St." sign and a smokejack for the coal stove. *Henry J. McCord*

 MODELING TIP

Crossings

Model crossings can be built in much the same way as those on the prototype. Start by adding the crossing material, then build the roadway to the crossing. The photos show an HO rubber-pad crossing kit from Walthers, together with the company's street-track panel kits. The crossing is painted black, and the street is painted aged concrete with chalk weathering. Prefab crossings of various types are made by Blair Line, Walthers, Woodland Scenics, and others.

 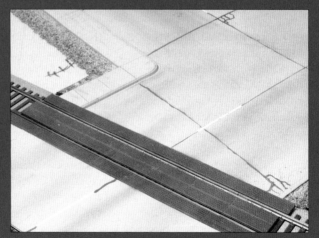

This Walthers HO scale rubber-pad crossing just needs paint, then it can be cut to length and glued over the track. Add road material (Walthers modular streets, in this case) and paint it for a realistic crossing. *Two photos: Jeff Wilson*

Most crossing guard positions were eliminated by the 1950s, but a few lasted through the 1960s. Here the watchman has his stop sign and red flag in hand as a Penn Central freight crosses Dutoit Street in Dayton, Ohio, in August 1971. *David P. Oroszi*

crossbucks of that period had black backgrounds with white lettering, with beads on the lettering. By the 1950s, reflective (Scotchlite) white panels became standard for the sign background.

An additional sign below the crossbuck lists the number of tracks (if there are two or more). Some railroads added a signboard with their herald, or added the railroad name to the signpost.

The 90-degree crossbuck has been standard for new installations since the 1960s, but older signs often survived a long time in service, especially along secondary routes, back roads, and rural areas. Main highways and streets are usually the first to be upgraded with new signs and warning equipment.

Crossbuck design in Canada was similar, but typically used "RAILWAY CROSSING" instead of "RAILROAD." Signs in Quebec (and sometimes in other provinces) had additional lettering in French. Modern Canadian crossbucks lack lettering; they're the standard shape but with red outlining on the boards.

Manually controlled crossing gates became the preferred method of protecting busy crossings by the late 1800s. This Illinois Central installation at East 57th Street on the south side of Chicago was controlled by an operator in the tower at right. It's shown around 1910. *Illinois Central*

Crossing sign style is a great way to identify the railroad and era being modeled, so check prototype photos for the period and region you're modeling for the most accurate appearance.

Watchmen and manual gates

Until the mid-1800s, train speeds were relatively slow, as were the speeds of the vehicles of the day: horse-drawn wagons and carts. As train speed and frequency increased, accidents also

A Wabash switcher approaches a manually controlled crossing in Detroit in 1960. This view from the operator's tower shows the gates, which have electric red lights and black and white stripes. The vertical rods are hinged; they drop down and contact the pavement to keep the gates parallel to the road surface. *J. David Ingles*

This Illinois Central crossing at Peotone, Ill., circa 1900, features an electric bell on a post next to the manual gates. The crossing tower is typical in that it has an elevated operator's bay atop an open frame. *Illinois Central*

increased, as people often misjudged train speeds or horses balked at crossings.

The first solution was a crossing tender or watchman. As trains approached, the watchman would move out into the roadway and flag down approaching vehicles. A red flag and/or stop sign on a handle was standard, with a red lantern at night. Railroads built small structures (crossing shanties) next to the crossing for shelter. These varied in design by railroad, and were typically small but with enough room for a couple of chairs and a coal stove.

Although staffing crossings was labor-intensive, it was effective. The jobs were often assigned to railroaders who had been injured on the job and could no longer do manual labor. The number of crossing watchmen dropped significantly with the coming of automatic signals, but some remained in service into the 1960s and even the 1970s.

The first patent for a manual crossing gate was issued in 1867, and

A bell on a post between the crossbuck and tracks serves to partially automate this Gulf, Mobile & Ohio crossing at Jacksonville, Mo., in 1963. The crossbuck features wood signboards on opposite sides of a wood post. *J. David Ingles*

A wig-wag signal is moving, with a red light at the bottom of the stop disc, on the Erie Lackawanna for an eastbound freight at Kirkwood, N.Y., in 1971. *Hugh L. Strobel*

Many wig-wags lasted into the 2000s, albeit with updated crossbucks featuring reflective signboards. This is a genuine Magnetic Flagman on the Soo Line in 1987. *Dean Freimund*

Crossbucks with alternating flashing red lights became the standard for automatic installations in the 1930s, replacing thousands of manual gates and flagmen. This one on the Monon has a beaded "stop on red signal" sign. *TRAINS magazine collection*

from that time through the 1930s, gates operated by a crossing watchman were common at crossings across the country. Early gates were controlled by mechanical cranks and linkage, with control levers on the ground next to the gates.

By the 1900s, pneumatically controlled gates became the norm. These allowed operators to control gates from inside elevated towers, providing better visibility and allowing a single operator to control gates at multiple crossings within his view. The installation often included a bell, which

could be pneumatically controlled or manually operated.

Manual gates were mounted on heavy pedestals at the side of the roadway. It was common to have two gates on each side of the tracks, with four gates at each crossing. Each gate was a "wishbone" style, of two pieces with the tips joined at the free end and split at the pedestal end at the pivot point. A heavy counterweight behind the pivot end made it easier to raise and lower the gates.

A rod hung down from the free end of each gate, serving as a stopper

to contact the road and keep the gate in position when lowered. Gates had hooks, allowing red lanterns to be hung on them at night. In urban areas, separate smaller gates were often located at sidewalks next to the roadway gates.

Manual gates began giving way to automatic signals by the 1920s; by 1935 there were about 4,500 crossings still controlled by manual gates in the U.S. (compared to 17,000 crossings with automatic devices). Manual installations lasted into the 1950s, but most were gone by the following decade.

This 1950s flasher on the Rio Grande also includes a bell at the top of the mast and a four-light vertical fixture with "stop" on the lenses. It also has a crossbuck with black background and white lettering, with beaded reflectors in the letters. *Donald Sims*

Automatic gates featured an A-frame ("wishbone") design into the 1970s, with black and white striping. This Milwaukee Road flasher includes an extra pair of lights on an arm, aimed at a side street. This is in Milwaukee in 1973. *Gordon Odegard*

Automatic controls

Track circuits had been used for controlling block signals since the 1870s, so the next logical step was using track circuits to control automatic grade-crossing warning devices. The first was in 1889, when American Signal Co. (which eventually became Western-Cullen-Hayes) developed a warning bell activated by a track circuit.

Bells were helpful, but the coming of the automobile and higher speeds for both railroad and highway traffic meant some type of visual indicator

was needed as well. The first widely accepted crossing signal became known as the wig-wag, which used a round target on a moveable arm with a red light at the center. When activated, the red light illuminated and the arm waved back and forth (powered by a magnet).

The first successful version, built by the Magnetic Signal Co. (and dubbed the "magnetic flagman") appeared in California around 1914. Other companies were soon offering their versions, and they began appearing on railroads across the country. Many

variations existed, with arms extending upward and downward, centered in brackets or extending on horizontal arms, and in many sizes. Separate crossing signs were typical on early installations, but many wig-wags eventually had crossbucks added to their masts.

Some early installations were placed in the middle of the road or street; this proved to be a road hazard of its own, so typical location became a pair of signals at each crossing, positioned to the right of each highway traffic lane just short of the tracks.

Griswold crossing flashers included a stop sign that rotated into position when activated. This is a crossing at a highway junction on the Duluth, Missabe & Iron Range near Virginia, Minn., in May 1979. *J. David Ingles*

Flashers on cantilevers are common at high-traffic crossings, such as this one on Soo Line in the 1980s. Gates became more common on these installations from that period onward. *TRAINS magazine collection*

Wig-wag signals were popular into the 1930s, when flashing lights and automatic gates became more common. Although many were replaced in the 1960s and later, there were still more than 1,000 wig-wag signals in service as of 2004. You can still find a few on back roads and low-traffic intersections, but they're disappearing quickly.

Crossing signals with alternating/flashing lights began appearing by the late 1920s. Typical installation was on a vertical metal post with a crossbuck at the top, with a red light and target on either side of the post. A common variation was having an additional set of vertical red lights centered on the mast with "stop" on the lenses. By the late 1930s, an additional set of flashing lights was sometimes added on a cantilever above the roadway (a common installation today).

By the 1940s, the AAR

(Left) Modern flashers have single-bar gates with red and white striping, and high-intensity LED lighting is standard for new signals. *Jeff Wilson*

(Above) As an alternative to locomotive horns, some new installations have directional horns mounted on posts at the crossing. This is at Mundelein, Ill., on Canadian National in 2008. *TRAINS magazine collection*

(Association of American Railroads) standard was for 8" lights on 20" targets, spaced 30" center-to-center. Size was increased in the 1970s to 12" lights on 20" targets, with target size increased to 24" in the 1980s. High-intensity LEDs are now used in place of bulbs on new signals.

The first automatically controlled gates appeared in 1936, the Western Model 10. Automatic gates are usually mounted on the same mast as the flashing signals, with a counterweight wrapping around the mast. Early gate design was similar to manual gates, with a wishbone-style (A-frame) two-piece blade and red lamps along the gate.

Unlike manual gates, automatic gates usually cover only half of the roadway, so each signal covers only the approaching lane on its side (with two signals at each crossing, one on each side of the tracks). Gate length varies to match the roadway and angle of the crossing.

Signal and gate details varied by manufacturer. One distinct version was the flashing signal with a rotating stop sign in a bracket below the crossbuck. These were made primarily

MODELING TIP

Crossing signals

Working crossing flashers and gates add a nice level of detail and animation to a grade-crossing scene. Working flashers are made in HO, N, and other scales by NJ International, Oregon Rail Supply, Tomar, Walthers, and others. They can made to automatically activate by either optical detectors or track circuits, or manually controlled by a toggle or pushbutton switch. See Larry Puckett's book *Wiring Projects for Your Model Railroad* (Kalmbach, 2018) for detailed information on installing working signals.

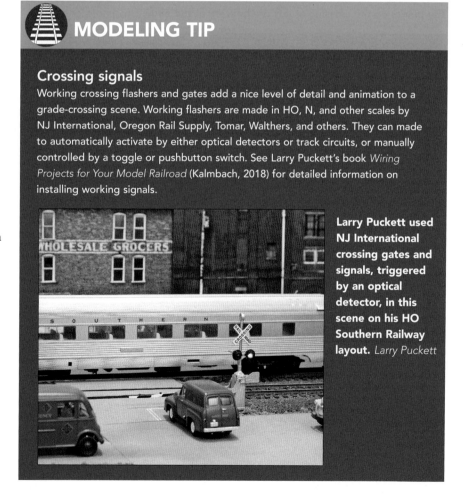

Larry Puckett used NJ International crossing gates and signals, triggered by an optical detector, in this scene on his HO Southern Railway layout. *Larry Puckett*

Early grade crossings were often just wood planks secured to the ties, as on this gravel road crossing the Alton in 1900. The planks on the crossing at left are beveled at the ends. *Library of Congress*

Many crossings simply have asphalt applied all the way to the rails, with grooves cut inside the railheads for the flangeways. *Jeff Wilson*

Some asphalt crossings have single timbers added inside and outside the rails. The planks on this crossing have shifted a bit. *Gordon Odegard*

by Griswold, but Western had a version as well. As a train approached, the flashers started and the stop sign rotated to face traffic. When the train cleared and the flashers stopped, the sign rotated 90 degrees.

Gates were painted with black-and-white diagonal stripes through the 1960s; red-and-white became standard around 1970. Around that time, gate style changed from the two-part A-frame style to a single-piece ("bar") arm, with the lights attached via a connecting plug. This made replacing arms much simpler. Gates began appearing at more and more crossings by the 1960s, especially on busy highways and streets, supplanting older light-only installations. They can be mounted on the same mast as the signal, or on a separate mounting post.

Activation technology improved as well. By the 1950s, separate circuits that required insulated rail gaps were replaced by audio-frequency overlay (AFO) circuits that didn't interfere with block signals. By the 1960s, these could allow crossing signals to automatically adjust to train speed and direction as well.

Crossing bells are usually included with flashers and gates. Through the 1990s this usually meant an electrically

This is a timber crossing using prefabricated panels. The ends of the planks, which extend beyond the roadway edge, are beveled. It's in Milwaukee in 1973. *Gordon Odegard*

Modular grade crossings became popular starting in the 1940s, using steel, concrete, and here, rubber pads. The sections are bolted to the ties; note the double spikes to secure the rails. This is on the Erie in the 1950s. *Goodyear*

operated gong-style bell at the top of the signal mast; after that, electronic bells became more common. Another modern variation that began appearing in the 1990s is a stationary directional horn mounted on a mast next to the signal, aimed down the roadway. It replaces the train horn; the stationary horn is louder for approaching motorists while producing less overall noise pollution.

As with block signals, automatic crossing signals require neighboring equipment sheds or cabinets. See Chapter 6 for more details.

Crossing materials

The grade crossing itself is critical, in that it has to allow open space atop the rails and inside the railheads for the flanges of locomotives and railcars, but provide a smooth surface for the highway with minimal shocks and bumps for vehicles (including those with small tires, such as motorcycles and bicycles).

Concrete-pad crossings are the most common for new installations. This is on a gravel road crossing on Union Pacific in 2005. *Jeff Wilson*

Early roads were dirt and gravel. To keep the material from fouling flangeways, railroads added guardrails inside the running rails. This allowed filling the area between guardrails with gravel, keeping the flangeways clear. Many gravel roads still have this type of crossing.

As asphalt became a popular paving material by the early 1900s, the same treatment was often done, with asphalt added up to the outside edge of the railheads and between the guardrails. (This didn't work for concrete, because concrete would crack from track movement.)

Wood timbers were the next upgrade for crossings, and they were used on gravel, asphalt, and concrete roads. Treated wood timbers were mounted to the ties, with spacers allowing for proper height, on the inside and outside of the running rails (again allowing a flangeway gap on the inside). Timbers were sometimes only used immediately inside the running rails, with the roadway material between; more common was to add timbers to cover the entire area between flangeways.

To minimize damage to crossings from dragging equipment, most timber crossings had beveled end timbers. The end timbers are extended beyond the edge of the roadway surface so that the crossing is wider than the roadway itself.

Timber crossings were the most common style through the steam era. Many timber crossings are still in use, although most are being replaced with more modern crossings.

By the 1940s, manufacturers were producing prefabricated grade crossings made from panels of hard rubber, steel, and concrete. The panels are bolted to the ties, and can be made as long as needed to match roadway width (crossing material generally extends 24" outside of the roadway pavement). Rubber and concrete are the most common materials for new grade crossings today.

The underlying track structure is important at grade crossings. Rail joints are avoided at crossings (and kept at least 6 feet away from their edges), because of the added track flexion at joints and the need to access joint bars and hardware. Longer ties are generally used (10-foot is now standard) for stability and to provide a wider anchor area for the crossing materials or panels, and track is double-spiked for stability.

Vertical curves are minimized as much as possible to avoid the tendency of long highway vehicles (especially low-boy flatbed trailers) bottoming out on the tracks. Since railways are often on a higher grade than roads, this often means adding fill to bring the road gradually up to rail-surface level.

CHAPTER EIGHT

Trackside signs

The fireman's view from a Penn Central E7 shows one of Pennsylvania Railroad's unique keystone-shaped whistle posts as the train approaches a pair of grade crossings between Kokomo and Elwood, Ind., in April 1971. A variety of regulatory and informational signs are located along the right of way. *J. David Ingles*

Lineside signs are not only interesting visually, they're also among the easiest details to add to a model railroad. Their style often helps identify a specific railroad and era. We'll look at how prototype railroads use informational and regulatory signs, how they're installed, and how their use has changed over the years.

Railroads have used many materials and styles for mileposts, including (from left) a concrete post on the Erie (61 miles from Jersey City, N.J.) in the 1950s; a stone post on Conrail's former Boston & Albany line (64 miles from Boston) in 1993; a standard metal sign on a wood post; and a modern metal sign on a U-shaped steel post on BNSF. *Photos (from left): Erie; Jeff Wilson; TRAINS magazine collection; Jeff Wilson*

Line poles (right) were convenient for mounting mile markers. Wood or steel signboards were affixed to poles; either a sign on each side or a double-sided sign projecting from the pole. *Kalmbach Media*

Posts and sign placement

Almost all lineside signs are mounted on a vertical post. Through the steam era, signposts were often treated wood, including square timber (4x4 to 6x6) or round posts (4" to 6" in diameter). These were nearly black when new, but faded to various shades of brown and gray and finally light gray as they were exposed to the elements for many years.

Iron pipe was another common signpost material, especially when used with cast-iron signs. The external diameter generally ranged from 2" to 3". Another similar material some railroads employed was used flue tubes, which railroads salvaged from steam locomotives. Sign boards could be bolted to the pipes, or with cast-iron signs, rest in fittings atop the post.

Old rail was also used for signposts on occasion. It might seem like overkill—the posts were certainly sturdy—but railroads often had old, light scrap rail on hand. The signboard could be welded or bolted to the flat base of the rail.

From the 1950s onward, U-shaped steel posts with prestamped mounting

POLE-MOUNTED MILE MARKERS

8" x 18" wood or sheet metal sign. Black numerals 6" high both sides

Back sides black

Screws

6" x 18"

Line pole

7'-0" to 12'-0"

Baltimore & Ohio circa 1906 (many railroads used similar methods)

Back sides mineral brown

8"

60°

6"-high numerals both sides

One stripe = ¼ mile
Two stripes = ½ mile
Three stripes = ¾ mile

1½"-wide black stripes spaced 3" apart

20"

6'-0"

White

Line pole

Some railroads used double-sided signs that extended outward from the pole.

Santa Fe circa 1951

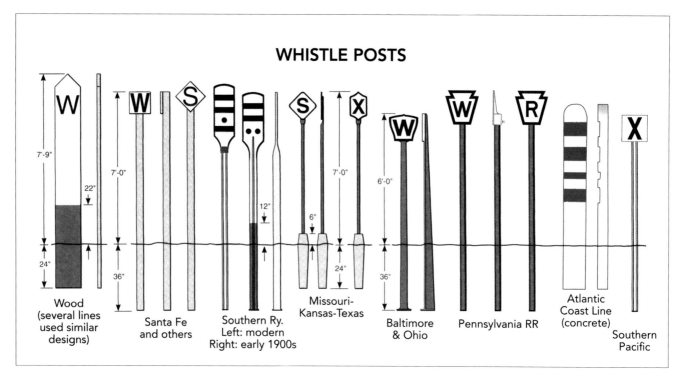

WHISTLE POSTS

Wood (several lines used similar designs) · 7'-9" · 22" · 24"

Santa Fe and others · 7'-0" · 36"

Southern Ry. Left: modern Right: early 1900s · 12"

Missouri-Kansas-Texas · 6" · 24"

Baltimore & Ohio · 7'-0" · 6'-0" · 36"

Pennsylvania RR

Atlantic Coast Line (concrete)

Southern Pacific

Assorted whistle posts include a wood sign on the New Haven; a cast concrete post on the New York Central; a cast-metal sign with open W, restored at the Illinois Railway Museum; a Southern Ry., sign with whistle indications; and a do-not-whistle sign. *Photos (from left): B.A. Bentz; New York Central; Jeff Wilson; Thomas E. Hoffmann; Robert S. McGonigal*

holes along their length became the most common for their strength, low cost, and ease of installation and replacement.

Each railroad specifies height and placement for various types of signs, and these dimensions vary quite a bit. Most signs are located 7 to 10 feet from the outside running rail, with a height of 6 to 10 feet above the ground line (this can vary based on the height of the roadbed and surrounding terrain). If in doubt, follow prototype examples and photos.

Mileposts

Mileposts (or mile markers) are more than just informational signs. Railroads based their timetables on mile locations, so knowing exactly how far a station or siding was from a train's location was vital to operations. In the steam era, many locomotives didn't have speedometers. Engine crews had to use their watches to count the time between mileposts to gauge their speed. And maintenance crews rely on mile markers to identify specific bridges, culverts, signals, line poles, and equipment cabinets.

The number on a milepost indicates the mileage from a specific starting point, usually the terminal in a city, the spot at which a branch or secondary main line diverges from another line, or the starting point of an operating division.

Marker placement is usually consistent, remaining on the same side of the track (often on the right-hand side as a train moves away from the starting point). Some railroads included initials of the city or point

This Santa Fe speed sign at Lamy, N.M., in 1974 includes separate speeds for passenger and freight trains. *John C. Lucas*

where the mileage started (Jersey City for the Erie post and Boston for the New York Central post on page 101).

The style of early mileposts was quite varied, with many railroads adopting distinctive designs. From the 1800s into the early 1900s, many railroads opted for substantial or ornate markers, including concrete posts or cast-iron signs atop metal poles. The concrete versions (Boston & Maine, New York Central, and others) had numbers cast into the concrete and then painted. Some used wood markers in a similar style, although they were not as long-lasting.

Placing mileposts on lineside poles was a common prototype practice. Since many railroads plant a specific number of poles per mile, counting posts is an easy way to determine mileage. Some railroads used additional markings on poles to indicate quarter miles. The drawing on page 101 illustrates how the Santa Fe, for example, did this by painting a portion of the pole white and used a mile number on top with horizontal black stripes below it to show quarter-mile divisions.

Since the early diesel era, the most common milepost design is placing numerals (usually about 6" tall) on a

Milwaukee Road used angled yellow signs to indicate speed zones, in this case 75 mph for passenger and 50 mph for freight. *Gordon Odegard*

The Atlantic Coast Line used a diamond-shaped yellow sign with reflector on top to let trains know to reduce speed to 60. Also note the "No Trespassing" sign at the end of a bridge. *Ralph Coleman*

plain metal-sheet signboard, mounted on a metal pole. These numbers can be horizontal or vertical, and are two-sided, often extending to the side of the pole. Black on a reflective white background is the most common.

Whistle and bell posts

Whistle posts let engineers know when to blow the whistle for approaching grade crossings. Most railroads signify this with a "W," although a few—notably Southern Pacific—used an X, and others have used symbols for the whistle pattern. And yes, even though steam whistles disappeared more than 60 years ago, they're still "whistle posts," not "horn posts."

The whistle signal for a crossing was initially two longs and two shorts, but most engineers would hold the last note until the crossing. This led to two longs, a short, and a long becoming official by the 1920s (and explains the early Southern cast-iron sign in the drawings on page 102).

As with mile markers, many railroads opted for ornate designs into the early 1900s. Concrete and wood in various designs were common, especially on Eastern lines. Atlantic Coast Line had substantial concrete posts with horizontal lines (cast-in and painted) indicating the whistle pattern.

Other notable whistle signs included Pennsylvania's cast-iron design, which featured the railroad's signature keystone herald as an outline for the "W," and the cast signs with open "W," used by several railroads.

By the 1950s, most railroads were

A leaning flanger post looms in the foreground as a Conrail B36-7 leads a train at Riverside, Mass., in 1983. *Tom Nelligan*

opting for simpler signs: a black "W" on a reflective white signboard, on a U-shaped steel post. Many older-style posts could be found in service much later.

Grade-crossing whistle posts are positioned about a quarter mile in advance of the crossing, but this distance can be adjusted based on maximum train speeds on a given line.

Whistle signs with an "S" indicated "station," which required a different whistle signal than a grade crossing (a single long whistle blast). These were placed from a half-mile to mile away from the station.

Related to these are signs with an "R," which indicates the engineer to "ring" the engine bell. This is generally when moving through station areas. They're usually the same style as whistle posts.

A variation on the whistle post is the "do not whistle" sign (page 102).

MODELING TIP

Scale miles and mileposts

If we place mileposts on a layout following true prototype practice, we wouldn't be able to add very many. A scale mile is 60'-6" in HO and 33' in N, so even those with the largest layouts would only be able to accurately have no more than two or three mileposts along the line.

Modelers have worked around this in many ways. Pioneering model railroader Frank Ellison came up with the idea of "smiles," equal to a tenth of a scale mile (about 6 feet in HO and 3 feet in N). Adding mileposts with that spacing or slightly longer will seem natural.

You can also further apply the principle of selective compression to mileposts just as with structures and scenes. For example, if you have three towns on your layout, and near the depot in the first town is milepost 53, you can add mileposts 58 and 64 between that town and the second town, milepost 68 in the second town, then mileposts 76 and 81 before the third town, and so on. By skipping numbers but keeping the numbers in sequence you provide a feeling of distance; that the railroad is going somewhere.

If you're modeling a specific prototype, you can use a timetable to find out what the specific milepost locations are for stations, and use that information to place accurate numbers on your modeled mileposts.

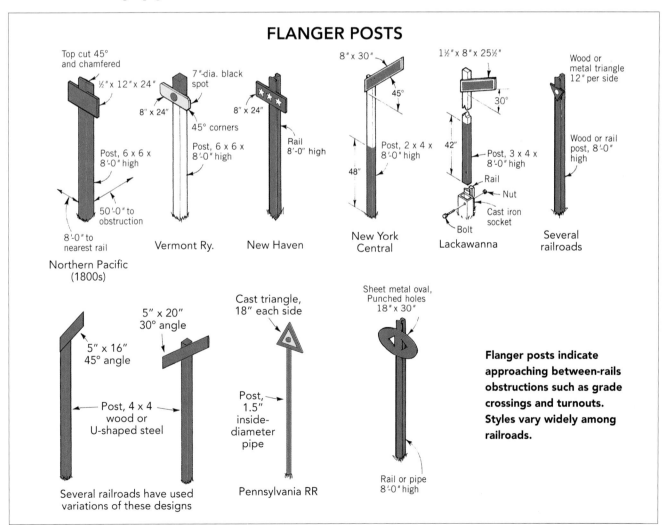

FLANGER POSTS

Flanger posts indicate approaching between-rails obstructions such as grade crossings and turnouts. Styles vary widely among railroads.

This sign marks the station location of Harrison, Neb., in 1975, even though the actual depot building is long gone. The scene is on Chicago & North Western's Cowboy line. *Merk Hobson*

P&N Junction was on Gulf, Mobile & Ohio's 4th Subdivision at milepost 35.7, 5 miles west of Delavan, Ill., and just east of San Jose, Ill. The site is marked by a wood signboard on a single post in this 1958 view. *Paul Larson*

Since the 1990s, many municipalities have enacted regulations prohibiting whistle use except in emergencies, so signs like these alert train crews to that effect. These are also used in areas where crossings have their own built-in directional horns (see Chapter 7).

The nice thing about all of these signs is that modern DCC sound systems allow modelers to operate bells, horns, and whistles in a realistic manner, so modeling these signs allows crews to use sounds realistically. You'll have to adjust the distances to suit model operations by placing signs closer (a few hundred scale feet instead of a quarter mile, for example).

Speed signs

Speed limits are important to prototype railroads, and they're determined by a variety of factors including the class of track (how highly it is maintained—see Chapter 2), the area (rural or urban), and operational factors such as curves and grades. Early speed signs could be ornate, but most are fairly simple, with the number (or two numbers if there are different limits for freight and passenger) on a rectangular or angled signboard mounted to a post.

Railroads generally follow their own standards and rules. Variations include the sign color, the shape of the signboard, and the style of the numbers. Black lettering on white or yellow backgrounds is the most common, with reflective backgrounds since the 1950s.

Speed restrictions are often in effect for sharp curves, bridges, tunnels, junctions, and urban areas. Again, these vary by railroad. Some lines use white as a background for the speed limit with yellow backgrounds for restricted-speed areas; others used letters to indicate this ("SR" for "speed restriction" and "RS" for "resume speed"), with advance-warning signs for speed restrictions at an angle on a yellow background. A plain green panel on a signboard indicates the end of the speed zone.

Temporary speed signs are sometimes used when maintenance crews are working—a plain yellow

board on a post. Trains will have also received orders and information regarding temporary speed zones via train order or other communication from the dispatcher.

Flanger posts

Keeping tracks clear of snow is an important part of winter operations. Along with a conventional plow, railroads use flangers, which have retractable blades that extend below railtop level between the rails. They clear ice and snow that can foul wheel flangeways.

Flanger posts are signs that alert flanger operators when they approach between-rails obstructions, such as grade crossings, turnouts, and guardrails. The operator, seeing the flanger sign, knows to raise the flanger blade until clear of the obstruction. Flanger posts were common by the 1890s, and could be found on any railroad that operated plows and flangers.

Flanger posts are easy to overlook. As the photos and drawings show, they have been made in a wide variety of styles, but the most common style is an angled black flag on a post. What makes them difficult to see in ordinary conditions—the black flag and (often) post—is what makes them stand out in snowy conditions. Some railroads used yellow as a color as well, or used other designs on the sign face. Another variation is adding additional flags to indicate to plow operators obstructions on the outside of the rail.

Flanger posts are generally placed about 100 to 200 feet in advance of the obstruction. This distance could be tightened a bit on model railroads (60-100 scale feet) and still be quite realistic.

Station and yard signs

Station signs are important in that they define specific locations as called out in timetables. The "station" does not mean an actual physical depot (although through the 1960s there often was indeed a structure at the location), but the location at the specified milepost location in the timetable. This can be at a town, railroad junction,

Many railroads used signs to indicate approaching stations and junctions. This is on the Milwaukee Road.
Gordon Odegard

passing siding, or other landmark. Station names are critical in railroad operations, where train orders and permission to occupy track are defined by station locations.

Where there's a depot, the sign is generally mounted on the building itself. However, for places where the depot is gone (or there never was one), the same style of sign will be found, but mounted on one or two posts. The style and size of these vary among railroads, but they are generally larger than most other lineside signs. Wood panels were common, although most modern signs are sheet metal, with black lettering on reflective white background.

Signs indicating an approaching station were usually posted a mile on either side of a station—"STATION ONE MILE" was a common sign. Junctions are also called out in advance in a similar manner.

Yard limit signs are important for operations, as they mark the boundaries of trackage where trains are governed by Rule 93, which allows trains to use the main tracks within yard limits, only requiring them to clear first-class trains. All other trains

Signs along a weed-grown Milwaukee Road track near Milwaukee in 1973 include a flanger post (black flags on a reflective white background on a wood post) and a crossing alert. *Gordon Odegard*

must operate within yard limits at restricted speed, watching for other trains and open turnouts.

The key is that yard limit restrictions may apply before the actual yard is encountered, and some railroads use yard limit rules on industrial tracks and other areas where there's no actual yard. Signs indicating the yard limit itself are often V-shaped, but some railroads use conventional rectangular signboards.

In addition, warning signs that a yard limit is approaching are generally placed a mile from the limit, allowing trains to slow to restricted speed. These "YARD LIMIT ONE MILE" signs can be triangular or rectangular, again varying by railroad and era.

Miscellaneous signs

Many signs relate to signaling, letting

Yard limit signs include, from left: a V-shaped sign on the Rio Grande in 1961; a rectangular sign on the Milwaukee Road (a metal sign attached to an older wood board), with a flanger post in front of it; and a triangular one mile sign on the Milwaukee Road. *Photos (from left): Denzel C. Allen, Jr.; Gordon Odegard (2)*

Track names and other locations or spots are often listed on signs, as here in this Northern Pacific scene at Lind, Wash., in 1943. *C.L. Tilbury*

Signaling signs—like this "BEGIN CTC" sign on a signal mast—are common. Also note the "no trespassing" and yellow angled speed limit sign in the background at left on this Milwaukee Road scene. *Gordon Odegard*

This sign shows where the boundary point of the automatic block. *Gordon Odegard*

 MODELING TIP

Converting photos to signs

Signs are among the easiest details to add to a layout using photography. Take a photo facing the prototype sign as square as possible. You can use any imaging software to resize the sign to your scale and fix any lighting or proportion issues. You can then print out the sign, mount it to thin plastic or cardstock, and add it to a signpost.

You can find photos of many signs (especially vintage) on various web sites as well. Be aware that although you can use images you find on the internet for your own purposes, you don't have the right to distribute them to others.

Lance Mindheim made this HO scale sign by taking a photo of a crossbuck on the prototype Los Angeles Junction Railway, printing the image, laminating it to thin styrene, and mounting it on a **post.** *Lance Mindheim*

This Northern Pacific advance-warning speed sign was made by scanning the graphic from an operating rulebook, resizing it, and printing the image and mounting it to a post. *Jeff Wilson*

Low-traffic rail crossings are sometimes guarded by simple stop signs, as here on the Chicago & North Western in the 1970s. This rather faded sign is illuminated by a hooded lamp atop the post. *TRAINS magazine collection*

crews know where signal blocks start and end, where Centralized Traffic Control blocks begin, and where grade crossing circuits and detectors begin.

"No trespassing" and "private property" signs are common in many locations, especially at bridges, tunnels, and other potentially dangerous areas. These vary widely by railroad, and many lines include their railroad names and/or heralds on the signs.

Stop signs are often used at crossings with other railroads, especially at low-traffic junctions where the expense of a tower or automatic signal isn't justified. As the name implies, trains must stop and make sure the route is clear before proceeding.

Other signs include clearance warnings, labels and names for tracks, and warnings for approaching the fouling point of another track. Some railroads post distance from stations or junctions in feet or numbers of cars—this lets engineers know when they're clear of opposing tracks.

Use the prototype (and photos) as your guide in adding signs to your layout. Distinctive sign designs can help place your layout in a specific era and region—and sometimes in an exact location.

Signs are often located at the point where equipment on one track with interfere with ("foul") traffic on another track.
TRAINS magazine collection

Bibliography

Books

All About Signals, by John Armstrong. Kalmbach Publishing Co., 1957.

Basic Trackwork for Model Railroaders, Second Edition, by Jeff Wilson. Kalmbach Publishing Co., 2014.

Classic Railroad Signals, by Brian Solomon. Voyageur Press, Quarto Publishing Group, 2015.

Guide to Signals & Interlockings, by Dave Abeles. Kalmbach Media, 2021.

The Model Railroader's Guide to Trackside Structures, by Jeff Wilson. Kalmbach Publishing Co., 2011.

Railroad Signaling, by Brian Solomon. MBI Publishing, 2003.

Periodicals

"Bending the Iron," by Tony Koester, *Model Railroader*, February 2006, p. 46.

"Bumping Posts and Car Stops," by Gordon Odegard, *Model Railroader*, April 1983, p. 100.

"Continuous Rail: A Challenge to the Engineer," *Modern Railroads*, August 1947.

"Derails," by Gordon Odegard, *Model Railroader*, December 1981, p. 78.

"Detailing the Right-of-Way," by Paul Dolkos, *Model Railroader*, November 2007, p. 48 (Part 1), December 2007, p. 66 (Part 2).

"Electronics Pin-Point Hot Boxes," *Railway Signaling and Communications*, April 1957, p. 19.

"Fighting Rail Wear," by Tyler Trahan, *Trains*, February 2020, p. 24.

"The Fine Science of Friction Control," by Eric Powell, *Trains*, June 2012, p. 18.

"Hot-Box Detector Gets Results on the Boston & Maine," *Railway Signaling and Communications*, November 1957.

"How to Superdetail a Turnout," by Lance Mindheim, *How to Build Realistic Reliable Track* (*Model Railroader* special issue, Summer 2009), p. 6.

"Instrument Cases and Where to Find Them," by Gordon Odegard, *Model Railroader*, June 1981, p. 74.

"Mileposts and Scale Miles," by Gordon Odegard, *Model Railroader*, February 1982, p. 96.

"Moving Targets for Switch Stands," by Bill Darnaby, *How to Build Realistic Layouts* (*Model Railroader* special issue, Summer 2006), p. 34.

"Not All Spikes are Golden," by Tyler Trahan, *Trains*, February 2019

"Paving a Way for the Railroad Line," *Trains*, March 2007, p. 25.

"Railroad Line Poles," by Gordon Odegard, *Model Railroader*, October 1981, p. 92.

"Railroad Speed Signs," by Gordon Odegard, *Model Railroader,* June 1992, p. 82.

"Right of Way Realism Through Civil Engineering," by Neal A. Schorr, *How to Build Realistic Reliable Track* (*Model Railroader* special issue, Summer 2009), p. 58.

"The Right of Way Tells a Story," by Michael J. Burgett, *How to Build Realistic Reliable Track* (*Model Railroader* special issue, Summer 2009), p. 14.

"Santa Fe Sentinels," by B.C. Hellman, *Trains*, January 2003, p. 52.

"Signaling," by Brian Solomon, *Trains*, November 2012, p. 64.

"Six Welded Rail Questions, *Trains*, December 2018, p. 20.

"Switch Stands and Targets," by Gordon Odegard, *Model Railroader,* February 1981, p. 82.

"Train Horns Fall by the Wayside," by Sayre C. Kos, *Trains*, November 2009, p. 16.

"Unlocking the Secrets of Interlockings," by Tony Koester, *How to Build Realistic Layouts* (*Model Railroader* special issue, Summer 2006), p. 58.

"Wayside Detectors Advancing Fast," by Steve Sweeney, *Trains*, March 2014, p. 20.

"Welded Rail," by David P. Morgon, *Trains*, February 1950.

"Where to Place Trackside Signals," by Michael J. Burgett, *How to Build Realistic Layouts* (*Model Railroader* special issue, Summer 2006), p. 52.

"Whistle Posts," by Gordon Odegard, *Model Railroader*, April 1992, p. 100.

Miscellaneous

Cant Excess for Freight Train Operations on Shared Track, Federal Railroad Administration report, February 2020.

A Centennial History of Alstom Signaling Inc., 1904-2004 (pamphlet no. 1364). Alstom Signaling Inc.

"Concrete Crossties in the United States," by John W. Weber, *PCI Journal* (Precast/Prestressed Concrete Institute), February 1969, p. 46.

Consolidated Code of Operating Rules, various editions

Federal Railroad Administration Track Safety Standards Compliance Manual, 2008 edition.

"Grades and Curves," by Robert S. McGonigal, trains.com, ABCs of Railroading

Manual of Uniform Traffic Control Devices, various editions

Railway Engineering & Maintenance Cyclopedia, various editions. Simmons-Boardman Publishing

The Tie Guide. Railway Tie Association, 1997, 2016.

The Track Cyclopedia, various editions. Simmons-Boardman Publishing

Various manufacturer catalogs, information sheets, and instruction manuals

Websites

railroadsignals.us
rrsignalpix.com
trains.com

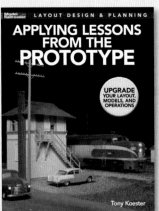
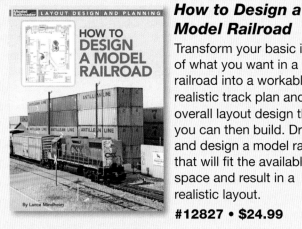
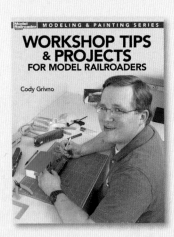
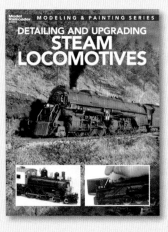